W9-BHW-328

# OHIO

# OHIO BY ROAD

# CELEBRATE THE STATES
# OHIO

## Victoria Sherrow

# BENCHMARK BOOKS

MARSHALL CAVENDISH
NEW YORK

Benchmark Books
Marshall Cavendish Corporation
99 White Plains Road
Tarrytown, New York 10591-9001

Library of Congress Cataloging-in-Publication Data
Sherrow, Victoria.
Ohio / Victoria Sherrow.
p.    cm. — (Celebrate the states)
Includes bibliographical references and index.
Summary: Discusses the geographic features, history, government, people,
and attractions of the state once called the "Gateway to the West."
ISBN 0-7614-0656-5 (lib. bdg.)
1. Ohio—Juvenile literature. [1. Ohio.] I. Title. II. Series
F491.3.S47   1999   977.1—dc21   97-15041   CIP   AC

Maps and graphics supplied by Oxford Cartographers, Oxford, England

Photo research by Matthew Joseph Dudley and Ellen Barrett Dudley

Cover photo: The Image Finders / Jim Yolajty

The photographs in this book are used by permission and through the courtesy of: *The Image Finders*: Susan
Spetz, 6-7, 124; Mark E. Gibson, 13, 20, 114; Jim Baron, 14, 19, 53, 56, 59, 60, 65, 67, 74, 104, backcover;
William A. Holmes, 46-47, 78, 102, 127; Michael Evans, 61, 80-81, 101, 106, 109, 136; Janet Cobb, 62-63;
Jim Yokajty, 77, 79; Michael Philip Manheim, 107. *Photo Researchers, Inc.*: Jim Steinberg, 10-11; Stephen J.
Krasemann, 17(left); Gregory Scott, 17(right); Frederica Georgia, 110; E. R. Degginger, 117; Rod Planck, 119;
Alvin E. Staffan, 120; C. O. Harris, 121. *Allen County Public Library*: 15. *Proctor and Gamble Collection*: 24-25.
*Ohio Historical Society*: 27, 28, 31, 36, 42, 97. *Ohio State Library*: 32. *Corbis-Bettmann*: 35, 51, 52, 87, 88, 89,
130(left & right), 134. *Western Reserve Historical Society*: 43. *UPI/Corbis-Bettmann*: 45, 68, 85(left & right), 93,
95, 129, 132. *Ohio Division of Travel and Tourism*: Doyle Yoder, 70. *Steve Shonk*: 71. *Jeff Iula*: 75. *Archive Photos*:
83, Bernard Gotfryd, 91, Reuters/Michael Mertz, 128. *The Image Bank*: Brett Froomer. 98-99. *Reuters/
Corbis-Bettmann*: 131.

Printed in Italy

1   3   5   6   4   2

# CONTENTS

# OHIO IS . . .

**Ohio is blessed with abundant natural resources . . .**

"The Ohio Country is fine, rich, level land, well-timbered."
—Explorer Christopher Gist, 1751

"A country beautiful and fertile, and affording . . . all that nature had decreed for the comfort of man."
—English traveler Morris Birkbeck, 1817

**. . . and people who pride themselves on being friendly.**

"[Ohio is] a place that commends itself . . . favorably and pleasantly to a stranger."     —British novelist Charles Dickens, 1842

"People in this town look out for each other. They greet their neighbors, old or new. If you need help, someone is there for you."
—Lifelong resident of Lisbon, Ohio, age 72

**Farms thrived on the fertile soil . . .**

"Oats, corn, and hay I always have on hand
For plenty I always grow on my own land."
—Popular verse in Ohio, early 1800s

**. . . and large cities grew on its waterways.**

"Cleveland . . . is an important and flourishing city. Commercial advantages are great, the harbor excellent."
—Artist John Kilburn, 1856

**In this one state you can find everything from beaches to ski slopes to the Rock and Roll Hall of Fame.**

"Ohio offers something for everyone."
—Governor George Voinovich, 1996

---

Ohio is both incredibly rich farmland and an industrial giant. It has given the world a dizzying array of manufactured goods. Ohioans invented wire flyswatters, flavored chewing gum, and the light bulb. Ohio produced America's first billionaire and its first law to protect women workers; its first shopping center and its first hot dog on a bun.

Ohio is home to bustling cities, lush pastures, and quiet towns. Add them all together and you have what a nineteenth-century Englishman, Lord Bruce, called "the most American part of America."

# 1 LAND OF PLENTY

The name Ohio comes from the Iroquois word "O-hy-o," which means "something great." To early American colonists, Ohio was the gateway to the West. Lying on the eastern edge of the Midwest, the state is bordered on the north by Michigan and Lake Erie. To the south are West Virginia and Kentucky. Indiana lies to the west and Pennsylvania to the east. This central location and the state's many waterways have played key roles in Ohio's growth and history.

## ROLLING HILLS AND WOODS

Millions of years ago, water covered Ohio. It eventually drained off, leaving behind swamps. Then came the Ice Age, when glaciers, some five thousand feet thick, covered two-thirds of Ohio.

Mammoths and mastodons, tall animals resembling elephants, roamed the land. Using their conelike teeth, they chewed on spruce trees that grew on ice-free patches of land. Scientists have found the bones of more than 150 mastodons in Ohio, some dating back ten thousand years.

When the last glacier receded from the area about 15,000 years ago, Ohio was left with four distinct regions. The west contains some of the most fertile land in the country and is part of America's Corn Belt. The south is dotted by rivers and rugged hills, which attract many hikers. Eastern Ohio is blessed with abundant mineral

*A scarecrow, arms outstretched, protects these cornfields from scavenging birds.*

deposits, such as clay, coal, salt, and oil. The north has both flat areas and gently rolling land, with productive soil that is good for growing fruits and vegetables.

The first settlers to arrive in Ohio found the region covered with lush forests, mostly of hardwood trees, such as chestnut, cherry, maple, hickory, and oak. Novelist Conrad Richter wrote that those early pioneers saw "a sea of treetops. . . . As far as the eye could reach, this lonely forest sea rolled on and on." Today, about one-fourth of the state remains wooded.

The horse chestnut tree, which is also called the buckeye, gave Ohio its nickname, the Buckeye State. This tree's creamy white flowers bloom in springtime. Later, these blossoms turn into brown nuts.

*Buckeyes gave the state its nickname.*

## "A LABOR OF LOVE"

In 1806, the legendary John Chapman, known as Johnny Appleseed, came through Ohio during his famous walk across the frontier. With sacks full of apple seeds, he made his way down the Ohio River to the Muskingum and across the state toward Indiana. Wherever he went, he planted seeds, so that future settlers could enjoy the flowers and fruit that had pleased him so much at his Pennsylvania home.

When Chapman died in 1845, Texas congressman Sam Houston made a speech about Johnny Appleseed's "labor of love," in the U.S. House of Representatives. He said, "This old man was one of the world's most useful citizens in his humble way." Because of Johnny Appleseed, hundreds of thousands of acres of apple trees now grow in Ohio. Their fragrant pink and white blossoms fill orchards every spring.

Fir trees also abound in the state. A popular story out of Wooster holds that the American tradition of the Christmas tree began there in 1847. August Imgard, a German immigrant, cut down a spruce tree and adorned it with candles, delighting his neighbors. The idea spread throughout Ohio and other parts of the country.

Ohioans in rural or wooded areas see plenty of wild creatures, including white-tailed deer, rabbits, foxes, coyotes, raccoons, opossums, and beavers. Chipmunks and squirrels dart across lawns during the warm months. The endangered bald eagle and barn owl live in Ohio, as do two endangered mammals, the bobcat and the river otter. Bird-watchers can spot cardinals, kingfishers, woodpeckers, larks, hawks, and owls.

## ABUNDANT WATERS

Ohio is blessed with abundant rivers and streams. In the north, the Maumee, Sandusky, Vermilion, and Cuyahoga flow into Lake Erie. Most waters in the south, including the Great Miami, Scioto, Hocking, and Muskingum Rivers, drain into the Ohio.

Lake Erie is the best-known lake in Ohio. Besides providing transportation, the lake yields tons of fish. One fish is so plentiful that Lake Erie has been called the Walleye Capital of the World. Most of Ohio's other lakes are small, but the state has many larger man-made lakes, chiefly in the east. Grand Lake St. Marys is the largest artificial body of water in the world built without machinery. It was created between 1830 and 1845 by damming several rivers. About 1,700 workers, mostly Irish and German immigrants, used pickaxes and shovels to move vast amounts of earth. Oxen and

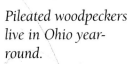
Pileated woodpeckers live in Ohio year-round.

Deer are the largest animals in Ohio's woodlands today.

horses carried the earth to the places where the dams were being formed. The lake is nine miles long and two and a half miles wide.

In this water-rich state, it's no surprise that many Ohioans enjoy fishing. Besides walleye, they can go after bass, pike, trout, perch, catfish, sunfish, panfish, bluegill, and crappie. "I believe I've caught just about every type of fish we have in Ohio by now," says one seventy-six-year-old fly fisherman. People also use the state's lakes and rivers for swimming, sailing, boating, canoeing, and waterskiing.

"People know our lakes and rivers, but many have never heard of our beautiful waterfalls," says Columbus native Jack Wheeler. The state's tallest waterfall, a ninety-foot cascade of water near Ash Cave at Hocking Hills State Park, dazzles visitors.

## DISTINCT SEASONS

Ohio has four well-marked seasons. Ohioans may complain about the state's severe winters, but some miss these seasons once they move away. "I never did get used to year-round sun," says a twenty-two-year-old who left Ohio to attend college in southern California. "It felt strange not to see snow or notice big changes from season to season."

Winters can be harsh in northeast Ohio, which receives most of the state's annual 2.5 feet of snow. Geauga County, east of Cleveland, averages nearly 9 feet of snow per year. "I dread the bad winters and look forward to spring each year," says Charles Galchick, who lives in this region. Sometimes the snowfall is so heavy that it completely covers cars parked on the street.

Spring, often brief, is usually rainy. About thirty-eight inches of

*Ohioans make the most of their snowy winters.*

## A WOOLLY WINTER?

While neighboring Pennsylvania looks to the groundhog to predict the weather, Ohioans rely on a caterpillar. At the Woolly Bear Festival in Vermilion each October, people examine the woolly bear caterpillar's black and orange stripes to see what kind of winter lies ahead. It is said that wide orange stripes mean that cold and blizzards are coming and that thin stripes promise milder weather. A parade, a costume contest, and caterpillar races are among the other attractions at this annual festival in northern Ohio.

*For many Ohioans, picking apples is a fall tradition that makes for good eating, too.*

precipitation fall each year. Summer brings thunderstorms, often severe ones. Ohio lies on the eastern edge of America's tornado belt, and generally a few twisters strike the state each year. In 1985, a tornado in western Ohio killed twelve people and destroyed many buildings, causing millions of dollars of damage. During the warm months, daisies, black-eyed Susans, violets, honeysuckle, Queen

Anne's lace, and sunflowers grow wild in meadows, woods, and lawns.

With fall comes dazzling shades of red, orange, gold, yellow, and violet to the trees. Many adult Ohioans fondly recall leaves crunching underfoot as they walked to school, the fun of jumping into raked-up leaf piles, and the scent of burning leaves at sunset. Autumn is also the time for high school football games, hayrides, county fairs, hundreds of festivals, and trips to local farms to pick apples and pumpkins.

## TROUBLED WATERS

Ohio began as a farming colony, but then large cities grew along waterways where industry and shipping flourished. As Ohio's population grew and its industry prospered, the state's land and water suffered terribly. Factories sent dirty smoke into the air. Chemical wastes, such as ash, acid, and cyanide, ran into streams and rivers. Other factories dumped oil, metals, and poisons from inks and dyes. Disease-causing organisms from sewage plants also fouled the water.

By 1948, the Ohio River was so dirty that people were not allowed to swim in it. Lake Erie was filthy. Algae grew so thick that it used up the oxygen fish needed to live. The algae on the lake's surface also blocked out sunlight, so underwater plants could not grow. "By the 1960s, Lake Erie was unofficially proclaimed 'dead.' . . . the air at times stank with dead fish," wrote historian Charles E. Cobb Jr.

The Cuyahoga River looked and smelled awful, too. It was strewn

# LAND AND WATER

N
W · E
S

*Lake* *Erie*

Ashtabula

Toledo

Lorain

Cleveland

*Pymatuning Reservoir*

Sandusky

Parma

*Shenango River Lake*

Bowling Green

*Maumee R.*

Warren

*Auglaize R.*

Akron

Youngstown

Findlay

*Sandusky R.*

*Berlin Lake*

Alliance

Massillon

Canton

Lima

Mansfield

*Charles Mill Lake*

*Killbuck R.*

*Sugar R.*

East Liverpool

Marion

*Scioto R.*

*Indian Lake*

*Grand Lake St. Marys*

Steubenville

*Great Miami R.*

*Alum Creek L.*

*Tuscarawas R.*

Newark

*Dillon Lake*

Cambridge

*Ohio R.*

Springfield

*Licking R.*

Zanesville

Columbus

*Buckeye Lake*

Dayton

Lancaster

*Muskingum R.*

Middletown

Marietta

Cincinnati

Chillicothe

Athens

*Paint R.*

*Rocky Fork Lake*

*Scioto R.*

*Ohio R.*

Portsmouth

*Ohio R.*

| | 0 – 500 ft. |

0  10  20  30  40  50  60  70
MILES

with steel-making waste products, sewage, trash, and chemical wastes. For years, oil had floated on the river's surface. This situation alarmed many people, especially when the Cuyahoga became the first river in the world to be officially declared a fire hazard. In June 1969, the river did indeed catch fire. Flames devoured two bridges in Cleveland, and some people began calling the city the Mistake by the Lake.

The Environmental Protection Agency (EPA) demanded that Ohio improve its waste disposal systems, especially along the rivers. New laws set high fines for companies that did not properly dispose of their wastes. Strict laws were passed to prevent factories and sewage plants from ruining the water. Gradually, these efforts paid off. Bass returned to Lake Erie, and swimming and fishing were resumed.

But while the water is much clearer now, the fight against pollution continues. Kevin Coyle, the president of the environmental organization American Rivers, says, "Though these waters may look cleaner, they may be more deadly." Water can contain certain poisons and bacteria yet still look clear and smell fine. Scientists must test the water to know if it is really safe. They are also trying to find out which chemicals in the water cause cancer and other diseases. Fish from the Cuyahoga River have shown high rates of cancer, prompting people to wonder whether fish from these waters are safe to eat.

While Ohio continues to struggle with pollution, it also strives to ensure the health of its industries. It takes hard work to maintain this balance, protecting both the environment and the economy. But hard work is a mainstay of Ohioans today, just as it was of the pioneers who settled this once rough land.

# 2 BUILDING OHIO

*Eden Park, by Lewis Meaken*

**P**eople have lived in what is now Ohio since before 12,000 B.C. They settled first in the southeastern part of the state. Then, after the glaciers receded and vegetation could grow, providing food for the large animals they hunted, people spread north and west.

## ANCIENT HUNTERS AND FARMERS

Ohio's early Native Americans hunted, gathered food, and grew crops, such as sunflowers and squash. They also left behind more than ten thousand mounds built from earth. The mounds served different purposes. Some were burial grounds for important tribe members. Others, which were made in geometric or animal shapes, may have been used in religious ceremonies. The Great Serpent Mound near Peebles in southern Ohio is the largest, most complex mound in the United States. Formed of stone and yellow clay, it is an amazing 1,335 feet long and looks like a huge snake. Scientists have dug up objects made of copper, clay, and stone from these ancient sites. The Adena pipe, one of the oldest Ohio artifacts found in good condition, dates back to about 100 B.C.

By the 1700s, the descendants of these early Native Americans were living in settled villages. They had been joined by Native Americans who had migrated from the central Mississippi Valley. The largest group, the Shawnee, lived in the Ohio Valley. The

*Centuries before settlers arrived in Marietta, Native Americans built the mounds in the background of this painting.*

Miami, Wyandot, Mingo, and Delaware were also dispersed around the region. Many Indian villages were located near river valleys in central and southern Ohio, which provided the Indians with ample opportunity to fish, hunt, and raise corn, squash, and beans.

They also traded with other Native American groups living as far away as the Gulf of Mexico and the Rocky Mountains. Travelers communicated with each other by marking symbols on trees along the trails they used.

## EUROPEANS ARRIVE

The French explorer René-Robert Cavalier, Sieur de La Salle is the first European known to have entered the Ohio region. In 1669 and 1670, La Salle sailed the Ohio River and was amazed by the beauty of the region. He called the river *la belle rivière*, "the beautiful river." Based on La Salle's travels, France claimed all the land between the Great Lakes and the Ohio River valley.

Fur trappers from both France and England soon descended on the area. Traders gave Native Americans knives, axes, cloth, woolen blankets, beads, guns, and gunpowder in exchange for beaver pelts.

During the 1700s, both the British and the French claimed territory in Ohio. France controlled the lower Ohio River valley, while Britain gained control in the north. Conflicts over land led to open warfare beginning in 1754, when the French and their

*Clergyman David Zeisberger led the Moravians who founded Schoenbrunn, the first white settlement in Ohio.*

Indian allies fought the British in what became known as the French and Indian War. When Britain won the war in 1763, it gained control of all of Ohio.

In 1772, a group of Moravian missionaries from Pennsylvania and Indians who had converted to Christianity founded the first organized settlement in Ohio. Schoenbrunn (German for "beautiful spring") was built on the bank of the Tuscarawas River near present-day New Philadelphia. These newcomers hunted, fished, and farmed the fertile land of the Ohio River valley. Their village thrived for five years but was abandoned during the Revolutionary War.

## RUGGED PIONEERS

While England ruled the American colonies, it banned settlement west of the Appalachian Mountains. That changed after the colonists won the Revolutionary War in 1783 and became independent. The new United States claimed all the land east of the Mississippi River that England had held.

Soon, settlers began trickling into Ohio. A group of men from New England formed the Ohio Company of Associates to buy land in Ohio. In 1788, on the Ohio River at the mouth of the Muskingum, they established Marietta, the first permanent white community in Ohio, which became a prosperous port city.

Other settlers headed west in sturdy covered wagons, making their way down muddy trails and across swollen rivers to get to the new territory. Some settlers were misled by land dealers who showed them pictures of developed towns where, in fact, there

## THE HAT ON THE SWAMP

In the early days of Ohio, many a traveler grumbled about the terrible roads. Tired men shared woeful tales about how they had made their way across dirt trails, ruts, and rivers only to find themselves in a muddy swamp. One traveler told a swamp tale to top them all:

While carefully crossing a deep swamp, he had seen a fine beaver hat lying in the mud. Why, what's that? he wondered.

Just then, the hat moved. Though the traveler was startled, he was too curious to flee. Instead, he poked the hat with his horsewhip. The hat fell off, revealing a man's head. The man looked up at the traveler, smiled, and said, "How do you do?"

The traveler realized that the fellow was up to his neck in mud, and he apologized for having knocked off the hat. "Perhaps I can pull you out from the mire?" he offered.

"Oh, don't worry," said the other. "It's true that I'm in quite a predicament, but my horse is right here beneath me. Together, we've managed to get through worse roads than this."

were only dirt trails. Newspaper ads claimed that Ohio land was "of much better quality than any others known to New England people." Soon, "Ohio fever" was sweeping the East Coast.

Although land was cheap, surviving on it was difficult. Settlers struggled against the sometimes severe weather as well as the bears, wolves, and weasels that attacked their farm animals. Many pioneers died from malaria and other diseases.

But the region provided a good life for those who could handle it. The wild territory contained plenty of game for skilled hunters. "The deer were so plentiful that they seemed to look out from the woods . . . to see what we were about," wrote one newcomer in

*In 1788, the riverboat* Adventure Gallery *brought settlers to the place where the Muskingum and Ohio Rivers meet. There they built Marietta, named after the French queen Marie Antoinette.*

1835. And the rich soil proved bountiful for the hardy pioneers.

One of the hardest tasks was clearing the wooded land of trees to make room to plant crops. The trees were chopped down and then the stumps were either burned out, pulled out with the help of oxen, or left to rot away. Frequently, settlers were forced to plant seeds among the dying tree trunks because there was not time to complete the job the first year. One traveler in 1839 wrote that the dying trees, "often scathed with fire and standing in vast numbers

*During the early 1800s, settlers changed Ohio forever. This sequence shows how they cleared away trees, built cabins, and planted crops.*

among the growing grain" gave "an air of bleakness and desolation to the farm lands." But finally the land was truly cleared. In 1800, an Ohioan described the joy of tilling cleared land: "None but those who have held the first plow, amid roots, stumps, stones, and trees, while the faithful team was pulling and jerking it along . . . can really enjoy the delight that the same plowman feels while holding the plow as it moves along without a root or stump to obstruct it."

The pioneers who settled Ohio were rugged and self-sufficient. They made their own soap, candles, and clothes and transformed wood, brick, and stone into homes and barns. People united for stump clearings and quilting bees. Children also pitched in. They gathered firewood, water, nuts, and wild grapes and berries. They helped to prepare food, milk cows, and churn butter.

Life in this new territory also had its pleasures. Children had fun swimming and playing outdoors, pitching horseshoes and running footraces. Their parents used whatever was available to make their children toys. Dolls were fashioned out of cornhusks, sometimes with heads made of dried apples. Deerskin stuffed with grass became a rag doll. The Indians showed the pioneers how to make a toy called the bull roarer from string and a stick of wood. Children swung the toy around until it made a roaring noise.

## CONFLICTS WITH NATIVE AMERICANS

As news of the fertile land spread back east, whites streamed into Ohio. Indians, fearful of losing their land, cried, "White man shall not plant corn north of the Ohio River!" But this was not to be.

Treaties were made, then later broken by the whites. Native Americans went hungry as whites killed game on their land. As the number of white settlers in Ohio increased, violent conflicts between the newcomers and Native Americans became inevitable.

Several major battles between whites and Indians took place in Ohio. A Miami warrior named Little Turtle defeated American troops twice, in 1790 and 1791. In the second battle, six hundred whites died, while the Indians lost only twenty-one men. But the fight over the land south of the Ohio River was not over. In 1794, the Indians were defeated at Fallen Timbers by U.S. troops led by General "Mad Anthony" Wayne.

The Indians had been relying on supplies and other help from the British to fight the Americans. After the Battle of Fallen Timbers, the British withdrew their support. With no hope of victory, the Ohio tribes signed the Treaty of Greenville in 1795, giving up their ancestral lands to the United States. By 1814, most Native Americans had been driven out of Ohio.

## GROWTH OF A STATE

In 1803, Ohio became the seventeenth state. During the following decades, Ohio would develop the excellent transportation networks that helped it become an economic powerhouse.

In 1796, Ebenezer Zane had built a road from the Ohio River opposite Wheeling, West Virginia, across southeastern Ohio. This road, called Zane's Trace, was the first highway leading west and for some time was the only road in the Midwest. Between 1811 and 1840, workers improved Zane's Trace, leveling it and covering it

# DON'T GIVE UP THE SHIP

During the War of 1812, the United States battled Great Britain for control of Lake Erie. In 1813, U.S. Navy lieutenant Oliver Hazard Perry was told to remove British warships from the lake.

That August, Perry left South Bass Island with nine ships, led by the *Lawrence*. On September 10, while anchored not far from present-day Sandusky, he spotted six British warships. Shots rang out, and Perry urged his men closer. The Battle of Lake Erie was fierce and bloody. One hundred fourteen of the *Lawrence*'s 130 crew members were killed or wounded. The sails were shot to shreds. Perry left the *Lawrence* in a rowboat and made his way to another ship, where he raised a large blue banner that said "Don't Give Up the Ship!"

Soon, the tide turned for the Americans. Expecting Perry to surrender, British ships came closer and two of them collided. The wind also shifted to favor the Americans. Perry opened fire on the British, and they were eventually forced to surrender. Then he sent his now-famous message, written on the back of an envelope, to U.S. Army general William Henry Harrison: "We have met the enemy and they are ours." This amazing victory raised the spirits of U.S. troops at a critical time in the war.

with crushed stones. It became part of what was known as the National Road. This new road made it much easier for travelers to reach Ohio, particularly by stagecoach, which hadn't been able to make it over the rough terrain of the earlier trails.

Railroads also helped open up Ohio. The first steam locomotive in northern Ohio was chartered in 1832. By 1860, Ohio had seventy-six railroads, some with many different lines. Many railroads were linked to canals. The Ohio and Erie Canal opened in 1832, connecting the Ohio River and Lake Erie. From Lake Erie, goods could be shipped through the Erie Canal, down the Hudson River to the Atlantic Ocean, and then all over the world. Many other canals in Ohio also linked important rivers to each other and to Lake Erie.

*In the nineteenth century, animals were often used to pull boats up Ohio's newly built canals.*

Technological innovations helped improve transportation. Steamships replaced flatboats and keelboats that had to be rowed or poled. In 1818, the first steamboat on Lake Erie, *Walk-in-the-Water*, left Buffalo, New York, and arrived in Cleveland amid much fanfare. The boat could travel eight to ten miles per hour, carrying one hundred passengers and three hundred tons of freight.

As Ohio's transportation networks improved, its small communities grew into thriving cities. Cleveland had begun as a frontier outpost. In 1796, Moses Cleaveland led a group from Connecticut

## POPULATION GROWTH: 1810–1990

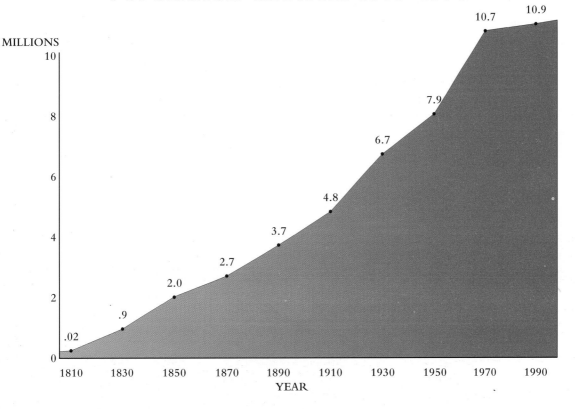

# THE LOVELY OHIO

Twenty years after the Erie Canal officially opened in 1825, Ohio had climbed from the thirteenth to the third most heavily populated state in the Union. The newly accessible land watered by the "lovely Ohio" had tempted many.

Come all ye brisk young fel-lows,— who have a mind to roam,— All in some for - eign coun - ter-ee, a long way from home;— All in some for - eign coun - ter-ee a - long with me to go, And we'll

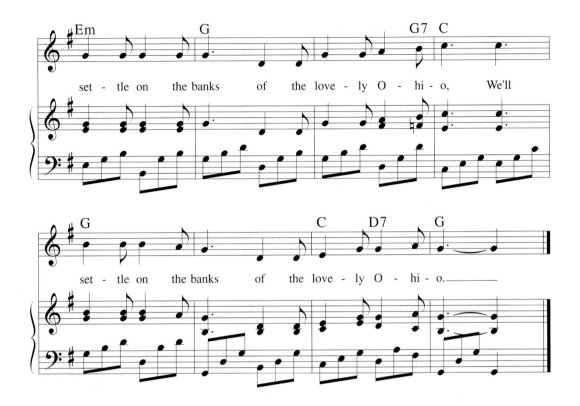

Come all you pretty fair maids, spin us some yarn
To make us some nice clothing to keep ourselves warm,
For you can knit and sew, my loves, while we do reap and mow,
When we settle on the banks of the lovely Ohio.

There are fishes in the river, just fitted for our use.
There's tall and lofty sugar cane that will give to us its juice,
There's every kind of game, my boys, also the buck and doe,
When we settle on the banks of the lovely Ohio.

to map out a city where the Cuyahoga River meets Lake Erie. Although Cleaveland never returned to Ohio, the new settlement took on his name, losing the first "a." A magazine article in 1853 praised the city's attractions: "So extensive is the lake that it has all the grandeur of an ocean view. The harbor of Cleveland is one of the best on the lake, being spacious and safe and sufficiently easy of access." Cleveland eventually grew into a major transportation and industrial hub.

In southern Ohio, Cincinnati became a center for shipping, manufacturing, and, particularly, meatpacking. So much pork was packed and shipped in Cincinnati—400,000 hogs every year—that the city was nicknamed Porkopolis. By the 1850s, it was America's sixth-largest city. Much of the state was experiencing similar growth. In 1800, only 45,000 people lived in Ohio. By 1850, the population had skyrocketed to nearly two million, making it the nation's third most populous state.

## THE FIGHT AGAINST SLAVERY

During the mid-1800s, Ohio became embroiled in the bitter arguments over slavery that divided North and South. Most Ohioans, especially those in the northern part of the state, opposed it. Ohio was home to many leading abolitionists—people who wanted to abolish slavery. In Mount Pleasant, Charles Osborn started the *Philanthropist*, America's first antislavery newspaper, in 1817. Another important abolitionist newspaper, the *Anti-Slavery Bugle*, came out of the northeastern Ohio towns of Salem and Lisbon. Newspapers such as these were just the beginning of Ohio's development into a center of abolitionism. By the late 1830s, more than two hundred antislavery societies were at work in Ohio, including one in Portage County with more than nine hundred members, which claimed to be the largest in the country.

In 1850, Congress passed the Fugitive Slave Act, which required federal agents to help slave owners track down escaped slaves. Many Ohioans bitterly opposed this law. Congressman Joshua Reed Giddings said, "Let the President drench our land of freedom in blood, but he will never make us obey *that* law."

Indeed, many Ohioans instead tried to help slaves escape. Ohio was the site of hundreds of stations on the Underground Railroad, a network of hiding places for people fleeing slavery in the South. More than 40,000 of the estimated 100,000 runaways used the Ohio route, making it the busiest "line" on the railroad. Levi Coffin, who hid slaves in his home near Cincinnati, was regarded as the Underground Railroad's unofficial president.

Oberlin in northern Ohio was another famous station. In 1858, several townspeople and Oberlin College students were arrested for aiding a runaway. They willingly went to jail to draw attention to their cause. While they were in prison, friendly jailers let them publish an antislavery paper. After they were freed, a crowd of supporters and a brass band welcomed them home.

Ohio played an important part in the Union effort after the Civil War began in 1861. More than 345,000 Ohioans served in the Union army. One of the most famous was ten-year-old Johnny Clem of Newark, who made his name as the Drummer Boy of Shiloh, the youngest military drummer in the country.

Ohio contributed far more than just men to the effort. Ohio

*Little Johnny Clem ran away from home to join the Union army. He became well known as a drummer boy after the Battle of Chattanooga.*

factories produced muskets, cannons, uniforms, shoes, tents, and saddles. Its packing plants sent meat and lard to the hungry troops. Families kept farms running while the men were away.

## BOOM AND BUST

After the North won the Civil War, Ohio continued to prosper. Iron and steel industries thrived in Cleveland, which lay close to large coal beds. Ships brought limestone from Lake Huron and iron ore from Lake Superior. Glass and clay production boomed.

Industrial jobs drew immigrants to Ohio from all over Europe as well as from other states. But while many business owners grew wealthy, workers generally earned low wages for hard, often risky, jobs. Those who became sick, injured, or jobless had no security.

To improve their lot, workers began joining labor unions. The Ohio Federation of Labor was established in 1885. The United Mine Workers of America was formed in Columbus five years later. Laws began to regulate big business and give workers more rights.

Ohio's economy continued to thrive into the 1920s. But then, in 1929, the Great Depression hit. Ohio was devastated. Factory orders plunged and businesses shut down. By 1932, 37 percent of Ohioans were out of work. In Cleveland and other cities, banks failed. People could not withdraw their savings, and businesses

*Many of the workers who helped Ohio become an industrial giant had to live and raise their families in run-down neighborhoods.*

could not meet payrolls. By 1935, the unemployment rates in some cities soared to 80 percent. Many farmers lost their land as food prices fell below the cost of production.

Ohioans did whatever they could to survive. Many grew their own food and made their own clothing and other household goods. A senior citizen who grew up in Flushing, Ohio, recalls, "Mom made our clothes, often out of flour sacks. She unraveled adult-size sweaters and used the yarn to knit mittens and scarves for us kids. Our big garden kept us going. We canned so many fruits and vegetables, even wild mushrooms and weeds. But we did have to go to the relief center for things like flour." Soup kitchens opened in cities and small towns to feed the state's many unemployed people. Relatives and friends shared cramped housing to avoid homelessness.

In the face of such hardships, many Ohioans welcomed Franklin Roosevelt's New Deal. After winning the 1932 presidential election, Roosevelt launched massive programs to help people survive the depression. Government-run projects put millions back to work building dams, bridges, public buildings, and roads.

But only with the outbreak of World War II did the economy really recover. About 840,000 Ohioans served in the armed forces during the war. While men fought overseas, Ohio women worked in defense plants and factories. Ohio turned out planes, autos, and trucks, as well as rubber and steel, for the war effort.

## RECENT CHALLENGES

The 1960s and 1970s were stormy times for the whole nation. The civil rights movement had made more people aware of racism in

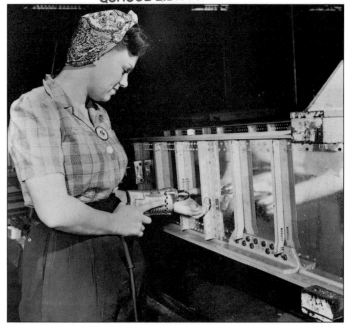

*During World War II, many women worked in factories building planes after men went off to fight.*

America. Violent riots erupted in Hough, the inner-city section of Cleveland, as African Americans expressed frustration over decades of inequality.

Bitter arguments raged during the 1960s over America's involvement in the Vietnam War. Many young people, in particular, opposed the war. In May 1970, during an antiwar protest at Kent State University near Akron, National Guardsmen shot at the crowd, killing four students and wounding nine others. The tragedy at Kent State shook the nation.

The 1970s saw a slump in the Ohio economy, caused by foreign competition, outdated equipment, less demand for heavy industry, and factories moving to warmer places in the South, which often didn't have unions, allowing companies to pay workers less. In the intervening years, Ohio has seen some hard times, but it has struggled to update its industries and develop new ones, which should ensure a bright future for the state.

# 3 MIDDLE OF THE ROAD

*The capitol in Columbus*

**A**n old adage says, "As Ohio goes, so goes the nation." Opinions in Ohio tend to reflect those around the United States. Professional pollsters call Ohio a "barometer state," a place to find out how Americans feel about political and social issues. "I'd say we're kind of practical, down-to-earth people," says a teacher in Cincinnati. "Nothing too far-out."

## INSIDE GOVERNMENT

Although in the frontier days Ohio's state government was small and limited in scope, today it plays an active role in business, education, the environment, tourism, and other areas. Like the federal system, the Ohio government has three branches: executive, legislative, and judicial.

**Executive.** The top state official is the governor, who is elected to a four-year term. A governor may serve an unlimited number of terms but can serve only two terms in a row. He or she proposes an annual budget, appoints people to key positions, and directs executive agencies and committees. Other elected state officials include lieutenant governor (who takes over if the governor dies or cannot serve), secretary of state, attorney general, auditor, and state treasurer.

**Legislative.** The General Assembly is Ohio's lawmaking body.

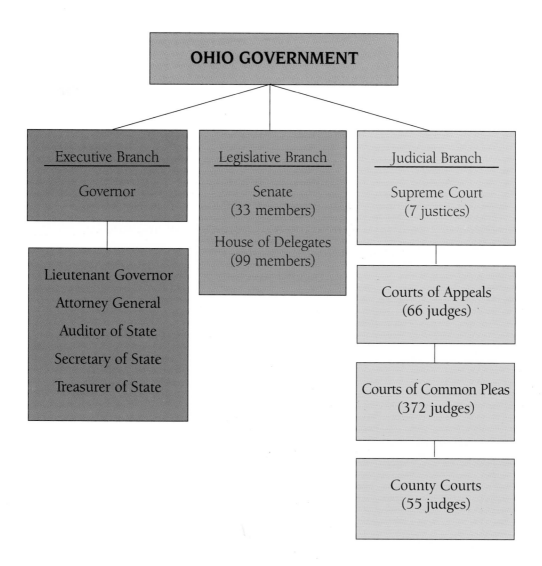

**OHIO GOVERNMENT**

**Executive Branch**

Governor

Lieutenant Governor

Attorney General

Auditor of State

Secretary of State

Treasurer of State

**Legislative Branch**

Senate
(33 members)

House of Delegates
(99 members)

**Judicial Branch**

Supreme Court
(7 justices)

Courts of Appeals
(66 judges)

Courts of Common Pleas
(372 judges)

County Courts
(55 judges)

It includes a senate, with thirty-three members who serve four-year terms, and a house of representatives, with ninety-nine members serving two-year terms. The General Assembly creates and changes laws and approves the annual state budget.

The highest state law is the Ohio Constitution. The state legislature can propose amendments to the constitution. Amendments can also be proposed by voter initiative or a constitutional convention. A majority of voters in a general election must then approve the amendment for it be enacted.

**Judicial.** The highest state court is the Ohio Supreme Court, which is made up of a chief justice and six associate justices, who are elected to six-year terms. The state has twelve courts of appeal, which are also headed by judges serving six-year terms as well.

Ohio has eighty-eight courts of common pleas, one for each county. In addition, there are county courts, municipal courts in larger cities, probate courts, and juvenile courts.

## MOTHER OF PRESIDENTS

Ohio has sometimes been called the Mother of Presidents because seven U.S. presidents were born there; an eighth, William Henry Harrison, lived there most of his life. Harrison became president in 1841 and died just a month after his inauguration.

Ohio native Ulysses S. Grant, the general of the Union army during the Civil War, became president in 1869. When he left office in 1877, he was succeeded by another Ohioan, Rutherford B. Hayes, who was replaced by yet another Ohioan, James A. Garfield, in 1881. A self-made man, Garfield had once worked guiding mules along the Ohio Canal and driving boats from the coal mines of Pennsylvania to Cleveland. Garfield was shot four months after he took office and died two weeks later.

Benjamin Harrison, who entered the White House in 1889, began the tradition of the White House Christmas tree. William McKinley became president in 1897. Shortly after he began his second term in 1901, he was assassinated. McKinley's love of red

*William Henry Harrison, the first of Ohio's eight presidents, died after just one month in office.*

carnations led Ohio legislators to make them the state flower.

Cincinnatian William Howard Taft was the first president to drive an automobile. A baseball lover, he started the tradition of having the president throw the first baseball at the season's opening game. In 1921, Taft also became the only former president to serve as a Supreme Court justice.

The most recent Ohio president, Warren G. Harding, took office in 1921. Harding was the first president to address the American people over the radio.

One Ohioan made history as the first woman to run for president. Victoria Claflin Woodhull of Homer, a suffragist and

*Victoria Woodhull was the first woman to run for president. She and her sister, Tennessee Chaflin, were also the first women in America to own a stockbrokerage.*

co-owner of a stockbrokerage firm, ran in 1872 on the Equal Rights Party ticket. During the 1870s, another Ohioan, James Royce of Newark, became president of the West African nation of Liberia.

## FIGHTING CRIME

Like many other states, Ohio has been striving to reduce crime rates and make streets and schools safe for citizens. Generally, people in small towns feel safer than people in large urban areas. A resident of the small town of Sebring says, "I don't worry much about crime, although it can happen anywhere. There's never been an incident in our neighborhood." City dwellers, on the other hand, sometimes suffer greatly from their area's high crime rates. In 1996, a family in Youngstown lost two sons, ages nineteen and twenty-three. Both were gunshot victims.

City schools saw rising crime rates during the 1980s, much of it drug-related. "At times, we have had police officers on school grounds, and we have monitors patrolling the halls," says a teacher at a Cleveland high school. Many urban schools have had similar problems, although the incidence of violent crimes decreased during the late 1990s.

*Police in Ohio have started new programs to combat crime and make neighborhoods safer.*

To combat crime, Ohio has created stricter sentencing laws for repeat offenders. Some communities are participating in a federal program called COPS—Community Oriented Policing Services. Under this program, police officers spend entire shifts working with the community without having to leave to answer calls. "The COPS give residents information on how not to become victims of crime," explains Warren police chief Albert Timko Jr. They try to get neighborhood residents involved in preventing crime. "We have started several block watch groups in high crime neighborhoods that have really helped," says Timko.

## INDUSTRIES, OLD AND NEW

During the economic slump of the late 1960s and 1970s, Ohio's once-busy factories sat empty, their machinery rusting. People called Ohio and the surrounding region the Rust Belt. "We were losing hope," remembers Bill Palek, who was laid off from several factory jobs during the 1970s. "Plants closing down, other ones laying people off. It was a terrible time for a lot of hard-working people who just wanted a job." Palek stayed in Ohio and did find another job, but some of his friends were forced to move south to find work.

To deal with the changing economy, Ohio manufacturers have become more diversified, and new service industries have developed. "We looked for new products that were in demand and have found new markets for our products," says a Youngstown plant manager. Although Akron was once almost exclusively associated with rubber making, today the city is a center for the trucking

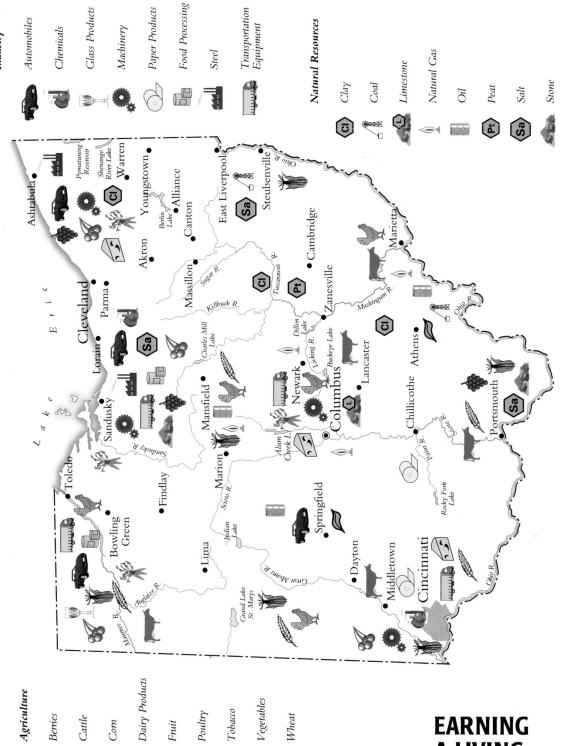

## Industry

- Automobiles
- Chemicals
- Glass Products
- Machinery
- Paper Products
- Food Processing
- Steel
- Transportation Equipment

## Natural Resources

- Clay **Cl**
- Coal
- Limestone **L**
- Natural Gas
- Oil
- Peat **Pt**
- Salt **Sa**
- Stone

## Agriculture

- Berries
- Cattle
- Corn
- Dairy Products
- Fruit
- Poultry
- Tobacco
- Vegetables
- Wheat

# EARNING A LIVING

Lake Erie

Ashtabula
Pymatuning Reservoir
Shenango River Lake
Warren
Youngstown
Alliance
Canton
Akron
Berlin Lake
East Liverpool
Steubenville **Sa**
Cambridge
Marietta
Cleveland
Parma
Lorain **Sa**
Sandusky
Massillon
Sugar R.
Killbuck R.
**Cl**
Tuscarawas R.
**Pt**
Zanesville
Muskingum R.
Ohio R.
Charles Mill Lake
Mansfield
Dillon Lake
Licking R.
Buckeye Lake
Newark
Columbus **L**
Lancaster
Athens
Chillicothe
**Cl**
Toledo
Sandusky R.
Marion
Alum Creek L.
Scioto R.
Findlay
Bowling Green
Lima
Indian Lake
Springfield
Paint R.
Rocky Fork Lake
Scioto R.
Portsmouth **Sa**
Maumee R.
Auglaize R.
Grand Lake St. Marys
Great Miami R.
Dayton
Middletown
Cincinnati
Ohio R.

industry as well as a leading producer of ultralight aircraft.

Ohio's attempts to keep up with the changing marketplace have been successful, and the state's economy has rebounded. Ohio makes more iron and steel than any state except Indiana. It ranks second to Michigan in producing cars and trucks and first in household appliances.

Ohio's factories turn out many things people use every day at work or at home—car parts, chemicals, electronics, paper products, leather goods, paint, silverware, scientific instruments, and furni-

*Factories in Ohio use new methods that can produce hundreds of tons of steel in less than thirty minutes.*

## TOYS AND TREATS

Young people throughout the world enjoy the toys and tasty treats that are made in Ohio. The Ohio Art Company in Bryan, near Akron, sells more than a million of its famous Etch A Sketches each year. The Kenner Company, which produces dolls, action figures, and many other toys, is based in Cincinnati. Hudson is the home of Little Tikes, known for its toys and children's furniture.

Many popular snacks also come from Ohio. Cain's Potato Chips and Snacks Company is located in Toledo. Marion is a major producer of popping corn. The first Cracker Jack–style popcorn, as well as the first flavored chewing gum, came from the Buckeye State.

Not to worry—Ohio has plenty of dentists, too. The first dental school in the nation was started in 1827 in Bainbridge by John Harris.

ture. Factories in Cincinnati make more playing cards and soap than any place in the world. The publishing and printing industries are also strong.

By the late 1990s, Ohio's economy was so robust that some businesses experienced a labor shortage. A manager at a McDonald's restaurant in Columbus said, "It's a constant problem finding enough workers. People can earn more money working at Honda," the auto plant located in nearby Marysville.

## PRODUCTIVE FARMS AND MINES

Ohio farmers have also had to adjust to changing times. "We've been farming for four generations," says a farmer in central Ohio.

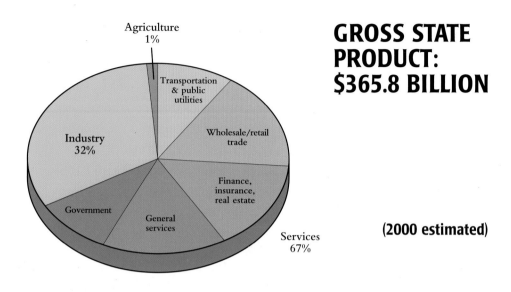

## GROSS STATE PRODUCT: $365.8 BILLION

**(2000 estimated)**

Agriculture 1%

Transportation & public utilities

Industry 32%

Wholesale/retail trade

Finance, insurance, real estate

Government

General services

Services 67%

"Yes, it's hard these days, especially for a small operation. We make it work because we love this life." They have made their farm more profitable by growing organic produce—fruits and vegetables grown without the use of pesticides. They sell to health food stores and vegetarian restaurants as well as directly to consumers.

Today, about 3 percent of Ohioans still manage to make their living in agriculture. About one-third of the cropland in Ohio is devoted to corn. Other important crops include soybeans, hay, sugar beets, tomatoes, and cucumbers. Fruits such as apples, pears, blueberries, strawberries, peaches, and sour cherries all grow well in Ohio. Farmers also sell eggs, milk, hogs, and horses. Ohio also produces more wool than any state east of the Mississippi River and grows some of the best wine grapes in America on the Bass Islands in Lake Erie.

Mining plays an important part in the state's economy. Ohio is the ninth-largest coal producer in the nation. Oil, natural gas, clay,

# RECIPE: FRIED APPLES

After the Civil War, a group of Ohio women wrote *The Buckeye Cook Book* for "Plucky Housewives Who Master Their Work Instead of Allowing It to Master Them." The book included recipes for such delicacies as skunk and raccoon. More typical is this tasty and simple dessert. Ask a grown-up to help with you with this recipe.

Oil or shortening
Firm apples, cored and cut into 1-inch-thick wedges (or, to be fancy, 1-inch-thick rings)
Brown or white sugar
Cinnamon (optional)

Put enough oil or shortening in a frying pan to just cover the bottom. Over low to medium heat, fry the apple slices until they are tender. Remove from heat and place on serving dish. Sprinkle with sugar or a combination of sugar and cinnamon.

limestone, sand, and sandstone are also mined. Ohio produces about 30 percent of the limestone used for building in the United States.

## PLANNING FOR A STRONG FUTURE

In recent years, Ohio's leaders have declared that education and programs to strengthen families are top priorities. The state assembly made funding available so that every child in Ohio, rich or poor, could attend preschool and have access to health care. In addition

*Sheep still graze on Ohio's farmlands. During the mid-1800s, Ohio led the nation in the production of wool.*

*Coal is Ohio's most important mineral.*

to serving children, these efforts created jobs, as new education and health care programs were set up.

Strong, well-educated people—these are Ohio's most important resource. Whether they work in farming, mining, or industry, it is Ohio's people who will shape the state's future.

# 4 LIFE IN THE BUCKEYE STATE

**B**uckeyes who move away often recall Ohio fondly. At a party in New York City, some well-known Ohioans were heaping praise on their home state. An exasperated New Yorker asked, "If Ohio's such a great state, why didn't all of you stay there?" Author James Thurber, one of the Ohioans present, replied, "Well, you see, out there the competition is too tough."

## AN ALL-AMERICAN STATE

In 1803, Ohio became the first "all-American state," settled by people from every state that already existed. Few of them were aristocrats. Hard work, practical ideas, and neighborliness meant more in the wilderness than social class. Most Ohioans today are, likewise, middle-class.

Ohio is average in other ways as well. Like the nation, the state's population is about 88 percent white and 10 percent black. Together, Asians, Native Americans, and Hispanics are 2 percent of Ohio's population. During the 1990s, more Latinos and Asians, particularly from India, arrived.

Like all Americans, Ohioans move around more than they once did. A sixty-seven-year-old woman in Salem remarks, "When my children were growing up, we had the same families on our block for twenty years. In the past ten years, eight new families have come

*Friends pose in front of their school.*

and others have left. Young people don't stay in their hometowns like they used to."

## FROM MANY LANDS

Although today about 97 percent of Ohioans were born in the United States, once people came from all over the world to work in Ohio. Irish, Swedes, and Norwegians helped build canals and railroads or took jobs as dockworkers. Italians, Poles, Germans, and Welsh manned the mines and iron and steel industries or worked in sausage factories or meatpacking plants. Wave upon wave of

# ETHNIC OHIO

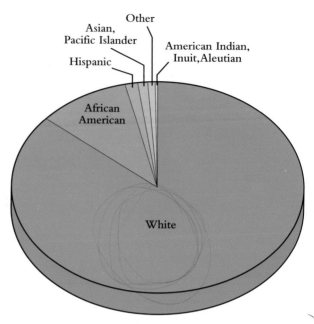

Other

Asian,
Pacific Islander

Hispanic

American Indian,
Inuit, Aleutian

African
American

White

immigrants came to Ohio—from Russia, Lithuania, Croatia, Slovenia, Serbia, Greece, Romania, Yugoslavia, Czechoslovakia, Hungary. The diverse origins of Ohio's people are evident in the names of its cities: Dublin, New Paris, Dresden, Geneva, Toledo, Holland, Oxford, Warsaw.

Today, the reminders of these diverse immigrants can still be seen in Ohio. More Hungarian Americans live in Cleveland than in any other city. It is home to a Hungarian-language newspaper and several of the finest Hungarian restaurants in America. On the menu are popular dishes such as goulash (a meat dish seasoned with paprika) and palascinta (thin pancakes served with preserves).

## TROUBLED CITIES

Ohio cities, like other cities across America, have struggled with poverty, unemployment, crime, and crowded, run-down schools with high dropout rates. During the economic slump of the 1970s, many businesses shut down, which meant less tax money for services such as schools. As such problems multiplied, many people who could afford to left the cities for the suburbs. Between 1950 and 1990, Cleveland's population fell by half.

When George Voinovich was mayor of Cleveland, he promoted various kinds of partnerships between government and industry to try to improve the city and keep people there. School-to-work programs helped high school students move into the workforce

*When factories closed during the 1970s, Cleveland suffered.*

by giving them on-the-job training while they were still in school. Cities and outlying suburbs took part in joint musical events and other activities. His administration also worked to clean the air and water. Gradually, programs such as these have made Cleveland a more livable city.

## AFRICAN AMERICANS

African Americans have lived in Ohio since its early days. Many came by way of the Underground Railroad. Thousands more came to Ohio for its job opportunities and found work in factories and defense plants. Ohio also offered educational opportunities. Wilberforce University near Dayton, founded in 1856, was the

*Carl Stokes was the first African American to be elected mayor of a major city.*

nation's first private university operated by blacks with a mostly black student body.

Although Ohio blacks have suffered discrimination in education, jobs, and housing, in the 1960s their opportunities expanded. More blacks were elected to office in Ohio. Robert C. Henry became mayor of Springfield in 1966, although just 14 percent of the voters were black. In 1967, Carl Stokes became mayor of Cleveland, making him the first African American elected to head a major city.

Today, African Americans continue to increase their presence in all walks of life, from politics to courtrooms to universities. A mathematics professor who grew up in Ohio says, "When I began college [in Cleveland in 1959], there weren't many black faculty members. That has changed a great deal."

## DIVERSE RELIGIONS

"A church around every corner," is how one Ohioan describes her hometown of 14,000 people. "People here are religious but respect others' beliefs."

Early settlers from New England brought their Puritan and Congregationalist faiths with them to Ohio. By the 1800s, other Protestant groups, including Episcopalians, Presbyterians, Universalists, Baptists, and Methodists, lived in the state. Ohio became an odd mix. Quiet towns with strict laws that forbade drinking alcohol or doing business on Sunday existed near riverboat towns famous for dancing, gambling, and horse racing.

Several small religious groups, including the Amish, Shakers, Moravians, Zoarites, and Quakers, came to Ohio. Today, more

Amish live in Ohio than in any other state. Traditional Amish families still live as their ancestors did more than a century ago, without motor vehicles, electricity, televisions, or telephones. They wear simple dark clothing and make most of the things they need and use. Their horse-drawn buggies can be seen on back roads in the northeastern part of the state.

The North Union Society of Shakers built a settlement in 1822 in

*The Amish know the value of working together. A barn raising means everyone lends a hand.*

# SEEKING RELIGIOUS FREEDOM

Several small religious groups fleeing persecution in Europe made their way to Ohio. Among them were about 225 Protestant separatists known as the Zoar Society. They came from Germany, where they had been persecuted for criticizing the Lutheran church, the dominant religious group in their region. By 1817, the Zoarites had earned enough money by working on the Erie Canal to found a community in northeastern Ohio. They built a communal society, sharing with each other whatever they grew and produced. They named their community Zoar, after a town of refuge in the Old Testament. The Zoarites built homes and barns, along with a tannery, brickyard, ore furnace, and workshops. Zoar was one of the first and most successful religious communal societies in America. It lasted for eighty years.

Historic Zoar Village has been restored and is open to the public. An 1850s-style harvest festival is held there each August. Besides music and good food, the festival includes displays of folk arts and crafts, antique carriages, and classic cars. Christmas in Zoar features strolling carolers, German holiday food, and tours of decorated homes.

present-day Cleveland. They believed in hard work, simplicity, and thrift. Men and women lived apart, and belongings were shared by all. The Shakers farmed and operated a sawmill, woolen mill, tannery, linseed oil mill, and broom factory. The community lasted until 1889.

Many Catholics and Jews also came to Ohio. In 1825, the first Catholic church in Cleveland was organized. Catholic immigrants from Ireland, Italy, Poland, and other countries found factory jobs in small towns and cities. Today, Roman Catholics are the single largest religious group in Ohio. Cleveland's first Jewish synagogue was completed in 1846. In Cincinnati in 1875, Hebrew Union College, with its Institute of Religion, became the first center of Jewish higher learning in the United States. Large Jewish congregations also grew in Columbus and Cincinnati and still flourish in all three cities today. Northeastern Ohio is also home to many Moslems, and recent Asian immigrants have brought their Buddhist, Shinto, and Hindu traditions to the state.

## ROADS TO LEARNING

The earliest settlers built schools along with their homes and churches. They erected one-room log or stone schoolhouses wherever there were enough children. Parents gave money or goods to pay the teacher, who often roomed with a local family. In 1825, public schools were established. Public high schools sprang up around 1850.

Ohio's colleges and universities are among the world's finest. In 1878, William H. Scott, an early president of Ohio State University in Columbus, said, "The University will be a glory to the state, a light and an inspiration to all who value and seek after the things of the mind." OSU is now one of the largest universities in the world, with a main campus that serves about 60,000 students. Dennis Mardas, a stockbroker who has lived in Columbus since 1959, is impressed by "the number of small and large colleges in our area, aside from Ohio State." He says, "In the past, people in other regions may have perceived Columbus as a 'cow-town.' But we have grown to be a business center, and most of all, an education town." Today, a half million students are enrolled at Ohio's more than 130 colleges and universities.

One of the most renowned is Oberlin College in northern Ohio. When it opened in 1833, it was the only school in the country where men and women of any race could apply. In 1854, John M. Langston, an African-American graduate of Oberlin, became clerk of an Ohio township, which made him the first black in the United States to hold elected office.

## SPORTS CRAZY

It seems that Ohioans have always loved sports. In 1893, Mount Union College was one of the first American colleges to form a basketball team. The Canton Bulldogs were one of the earliest football teams. In 1869, the Cincinnati Red Stockings became the first professional baseball team. They traveled 11,877 miles in one season, playing any team that challenged them. The Red Stockings won fifty-six of the fifty-seven games they played; the other game ended in a tie. Said the team's proud manager, "I'd rather be

*Ohioans of all ages love football.*

president of the Cincinnati Reds than of the United States." When the first pro baseball league, the National Association (later the National League), was formed in 1871, the season opened in Cleveland. Today, Ohio baseball fans continue to cheer on the Cincinnati Reds and the Cleveland Indians. Football fans root for the Cincinnati Bengals and pack the stadium at Ohio State University, where the OSU Buckeyes are a perennial college powerhouse.

# A RACE JUST FOR KIDS

Each August, Akron, Ohio, hosts the All-American Soap Box Derby. Young people between ages nine and sixteen from all over the world compete in this downhill race.

The Soap Box Derby began in 1934 during the Great Depression. Young people used wooden crates that had contained boxes of soap to build their cars. Today, they can buy approved kits that can be assembled into racers. Strict standards regulate the size, weight, and cost of the cars.

About three hundred contestants take part each year, driving their homemade, engineless cars that are powered by gravity down the hill at Derby Downs. Winners receive college scholarships and other prizes.

In 1994, Ohioan Danielle Del Ferraro, age thirteen, became the first two-time winner in the history of the derby. She won the Masters division, after having triumphed in the Kit division the previous year.

## FAIRS AND FESTIVALS

Want to see a Mohican powwow, a mock Civil War battle, a Slavic folk dance, Scottish bagpipers, a hydroplane race, or a motorcycle rodeo? Would you like to pitch horseshoes, stomp grapes, or stir apple butter over an open fire? Taste a zucchini milkshake or pumpkin taffy? You can do all this and more at the fairs and festivals held in Ohio. These events celebrate the history, ethnic roots, and special features of each locale.

Many Ohio festivals focus on food—everything from corn, apples, and strawberries to honey, black walnuts, and walleyes. Circleville, near Columbus, is renowned for its annual fall Pumpkin Show. An amazing pumpkin tower uses 250,000 pounds of pumpkins, gourds, and squashes. Bands serenade visitors as they applaud magic acts, admire arts and crafts, and view the world's largest pumpkin pie, made with eighty-four pounds of cooked pumpkin. Among the many pumpkin snacks are muffins, cakes, cookies, candies, and ice cream. The Ohio Honey Festival is held in August in Hamilton. More than two hundred booths offer samples of various kinds of honey for sale. During the festival, a beekeeper amazes visitors by creating a "living bee beard" on his face. A seven-year-old who saw the bee beard says, "I couldn't believe that was *really* bees until I saw him close up and they were!"

Festivals also celebrate the diverse cultures that enrich Ohio. The Puerto Rican Cultural Festival takes place in Cleveland each summer. The Slavic Village Harvest Festival, also in Cleveland, features a

*Young Iroquois dancers carry on the traditions of their ancestors.*

kielbasa (a type of sausage) cook-off. Sugarcreek is the site of the Ohio Swiss Festival. Alpine charm and Swiss-style buildings attract visitors to this city year-round. The festival features music, costumed dancers, traditional foods, a Swiss wrestling match, and a stone-tossing contest.

Each fall, Kirtland holds the Ohio Wine Festival. Visitors can tour local wineries and watch wine-making contests. In their bare feet, people can stomp barrels filled with grapes. The Geneva Grape Jamboree in Geneva-on-the-Lake also celebrates the local harvest

*Pumpkins form a lofty pyramid at Circleville's annual pumpkin festival.*

*A performance by a mariachi band delights spectators at the 1996 National Folk Festival in Dayton.*

with music, dancing, parades, contests, tours of wineries, grape stomping, and displays of grape products.

Besides such festivals, Ohioans can be found enjoying themselves at church suppers, school picnics, city street fairs, Fourth of July parades, and other community gatherings. "You can have your fancy balls and opening nights," says one native Ohioan. "For me, this is where the real fun is."

# 5 HUMAN RICHES

**W**hile describing his native Ohio, author Louis Bromfield once said, "It is probably the richest area of its size in the world." Bromfield meant the natural resources of the state, but Ohio is also rich in human resources.

## LEADING THE WAY

The great Shawnee chief Tecumseh was born around 1768 near present-day Springfield. During his youth, Europeans moved onto the Ohio frontier, pushing the Shawnee west. Tecumseh led a group of Indians who wanted to keep their traditions and reject white ways.

Early in the 1800s, Tecumseh warned Indian leaders, "The annihilation of our race is at hand unless we unite in one common cause against the common foe." In 1811, he asked, "Where today is the Pequod? Where the Narragansetts, the Mohawks, Poca-hokets, and many other once powerful tribes of our race? They have vanished before the [greed] and oppression of the white men, as snow before a summer sun."

Tecumseh was respected by both whites and Indians for his courage and statesmanship. William Henry Harrison, governor of Indiana Territory and later U.S. president, called him "one of those uncommon geniuses." Despite his efforts, the Shawnee and other

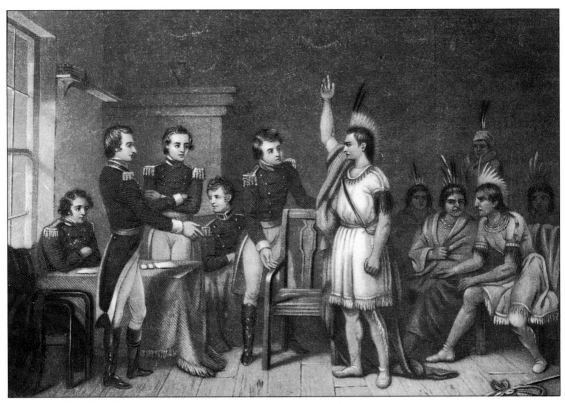

*Tecumseh urged Indians not to sell any land, saying, "Why not sell the air, the great sea, as well as the earth? Did not the great Spirit make them all for the use of his children?"*

tribes lost their ancestral lands. Tecumseh died in 1813 while fighting with British troops against Americans at the Battle of the Thames in Ontario, Canada.

Gloria Steinem has long been one of America's leading advocates for women's rights. She grew up in a poor family in Toledo. As a child, she learned to be both independent and concerned for others, because she often had to care for both herself and her mother, who was mentally ill.

Steinem received a scholarship to attend prestigious Smith

College in Massachusetts. After graduating, she moved to New York City and became a journalist, writing about subjects ranging from fashion to travel to politics. Tall and slim, Steinem also appeared in magazines as a model.

In 1972, Steinem founded *Ms.* magazine. Instead of focusing on makeup, clothing, hairstyles, or cooking, *Ms.* discusses political, social, and economic issues important to women. The Ms. Foundation works for laws and policies that give women equal rights. Today, Steinem continues to be a popular speaker and writer, discussing any issue, big or small, that affects women.

Although Lillian Wald was born into a wealthy family in 1867, she dedicated her life to helping the less fortunate. As a child in Cincinnati, she saw her mother give food and money to needy people who came to their door. Wald received a fine education, and she traveled and went to museums, concerts, teas, and dances.

She could have continued her comfortable life, but instead she became a nurse in New York City. One day she was teaching a class for immigrant women in a poor section of the city when a frightened young girl ran in and begged for a nurse to help her mother. Wald followed the girl home and was shocked by her dark, dingy apartment. The family had no food and used wooden planks for beds. Wald decided that people in this area needed nurses who would make home visits.

She set up a visiting nurse service in a neighborhood building, where she and other nurses lived. Wald convinced wealthy friends and concerned citizens to donate their time and money. Besides running the free visiting nurse service, the Henry Street Settlement House, as it was called, offered educational and social programs.

Feminist, editor, and author Gloria Steinem (right) poses with Ms. magazine's cofounder, Pat Carbine, before the cover for the fifth-anniversary issue.

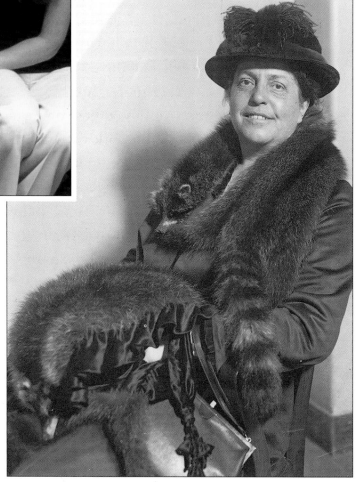

Lillian Wald—nurse, social worker, and humanitarian—was once asked how she had achieved so much during her life. "I really love people," she replied.

Wald and her nurses cared for the sick and injured and for pregnant women and newborns. They taught people ways to stay healthy and prevent illnesses from spreading.

In 1902, Wald persuaded New York officials to place nurses in the public schools. This idea spread all over the United States and around the world. Until her death in 1940, Wald continued to fight for laws to help the poor, especially children.

## INVENTORS AND INDUSTRIALISTS

Inventor Thomas Alva Edison was born in Milan, Ohio, in 1847. He quit school after only a few months because his teacher complained that he was too rowdy and called him a "dunce." Instead, he learned at home with his mother. At age twelve, he began selling newspapers. During his free time, he conducted experiments with printing presses and electrical devices.

Edison eventually moved to New York and began working at a telegraph company, where he developed better equipment and ways of sending messages. By 1876, he had saved enough money to build his own research laboratory in Menlo Park, New Jersey. A year later, he unveiled the phonograph. In 1879, he came out with the electric light bulb. Edison's other gifts to the world include the motion picture machine and the storage battery. In all, he patented more than a thousand inventions. Once, somebody mentioned to Edison that he had experienced many failures before he finally invented the light bulb. Edison replied that he did not view these as "failures"; rather, the invention took "one thousand steps."

The industrialist John D. Rockefeller was born in New York State

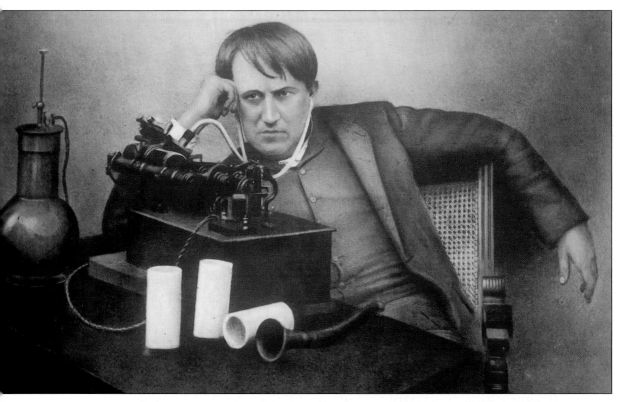

*Inventor Thomas Edison attributed his success to hard work and persistence, saying, "Genius is 1 percent inspiration and 99 percent perspiration."*

in 1839. His family moved to Cleveland in 1853, and Rockefeller attended public schools there. When he was sixteen years old, he began working as a bookkeeper.

During his twenties, he saw that crude oil was destined to replace the costly whale oil that was used to light lamps. He started a business with Samuel Andrews, who had developed an inexpensive method of refining crude oil. By 1870, this small company had grown into the Standard Oil Company of Ohio, which would eventually control America's oil industry and make Rockefeller America's first billionaire.

*John D. Rockefeller was the first billionaire in the United States.*

Rockefeller remained a prominent businessman until his death in 1937. By that time, he had donated about $550 million to charities. Through the family trusts, his descendants continue to contribute millions of dollars to various causes, including medical research, education, and the arts.

## PIONEERS OF AIR AND SPACE

Growing up in Dayton, Wilbur and Orville Wright were fascinated by aviation. They made kites and toy helicopters and studied how birds rise by flying into the wind. While running a bicycle shop, the Wright brothers built gas engines, gliders, and wind tunnels. They tested their gliders in the fields outside of Dayton and then tried out larger gliders on the wide, windy beaches of Kitty Hawk, North Carolina.

On December 17, 1903, at Kitty Hawk, the Wrights flew the first plane with an engine. Winds from the north blew at twenty to

*To show Americans that airplanes really could fly, the Wright brothers, shown here working on a plane, staged air shows around the country.*

twenty-five miles per hour as Orville climbed aboard. The rope holding the craft on the ground was untied, and the plane glided. It reached a speed of seven to nine miles per hour as it rose into the air. The famous flight lasted twelve seconds, as did a second flight with Wilbur as pilot. By the fourth trial, Wilbur flew 852 feet and stayed aloft for fifty-nine seconds. Orville called this the first time in history "in which a machine carrying a man had raised itself by its own power into the air in full flight." Today, the Wright Cycle Shop in Dayton replicates the place where the Wrights made new bicycles and repaired old ones while working on their experiments.

Ohioans also helped take America into the Space Age. On February 20, 1962, astronaut John Glenn became the first American to orbit the earth. Glenn, a Cambridge native, was born in 1921. After the bombing of Pearl Harbor, he joined the U.S. Navy for flight training. Glenn piloted 149 combat missions with the U.S. Marine Corps in World War II and the Korean War.

Glenn was one of the original seven astronauts in the National Aeronautics and Space Administration program. After his career as an astronaut ended, he entered politics. He won election to the U.S. Congress as a Democratic senator from Ohio in 1974 and served until his retirement in 1998.

Ohioan Neil Armstrong was the first person to walk on the moon. On July 20, 1969, 600 million television viewers heard him say, "That's one small step for a man, one giant leap for mankind." Before becoming an astronaut, Armstrong had been a navy pilot during the Korean War and then a civilian test pilot. He began astronaut training in 1962, and then as commander of the *Apollo 11* mission he made his famous step.

*Nobel Prize–winner Toni Morrison is both a novelist and playwright.*

## CREATIVE SPARKS

Ohioans apply their creativity to the arts as well as science and invention. All kinds of music can be heard in the state. Cleveland, Cincinnati, and Columbus boast world-class symphony orchestras.

Contemporary music also thrives in Ohio. Cleveland disc jockey Allen Freed coined the phrase "rock and roll" in the 1950s. Ohio has its own official state rock song: "Hang On Sloopy," which was written and recorded in the 1960s by a Dayton band called the McCoys.

Toni Morrison, the author of several acclaimed novels, was the first African American to receive the prestigious Nobel Prize for literature. This international award came in 1993 after the publication of her novel *Beloved*, the story of an escaped slave living in post–Civil War Ohio. Her first book, *The Bluest Eye*, was set in her northern Ohio hometown of Lorain. Morrison's novels have been praised for their brilliant language, strong emotions, and universal themes.

Morrison was born in 1931 in Lorain, where her father was a shipyard welder. She graduated from high school in 1949, then earned degrees at Howard and Cornell Universities and began teaching college English. Morrison later moved to New York City, where she began writing fiction. As a writer, Morrison has explored the black experience in different regions of America. In 1989, Morrison became a professor at Princeton University, where she continues to combine teaching and writing.

## GOOD SPORTS

"The instant I stood inside that stadium, I felt something I'd never felt before. Oh, it was awesome and beautiful . . . I knew I'd win there. I knew I'd break the world's record there," said nineteen-year-old Jesse Owens when he first arrived at Ohio State University. Owens did break numerous records and later became the first person to win four gold medals at a summer Olympics.

James Cleveland Owens was born in Alabama in 1913 but grew up in Cleveland. Tall and fast, he became a star athlete at East Technical High School. After he saw Owens run at a college meet, Big Ten sports commissioner Kenneth Wilson said, "He is a floating wonder, just like he had wings."

At the 1936 Olympics, Owens thrilled sports lovers and freedom-loving people around the world. Adolf Hitler's Nazi party ruled Germany, the nation hosting the games. The Nazis claimed that Germans were a superior race, while Jews, Gypsies, Poles, and people of color were inferior, even "subhuman." By defeating his German competitors, the "Buckeye Bullet" proved the Nazis wrong. His poise and friendliness, along with his athletic grace, made him a national hero.

*Jesse Owens once said that it takes "determination, dedication, self-discipline, and effort" to make dreams come true.*

# A DIFFERENT KIND OF HERO

One famous sports figure from Ohio is remembered not for his athletic skill but for helping integrate his sport. In 1945, as general manager of the Brooklyn Dodgers, Branch Rickey recruited Jackie Robinson to break the "color line" that barred black players from major league baseball.

Rickey was born in Little California, a small town in southern Ohio. He loved baseball, but his talent took him no further than the minor leagues. He went on to become a manager, however.

While coaching at Ohio Wesleyan University, he saw the pain racism caused the team's African-American first baseman, Charles Thomas. When the team was traveling, Thomas was often asked to leave hotels and restaurants, because they refused to serve blacks. Rickey later said, "I vowed that I would always do whatever I could to see that other Americans did not have to face the bitter humiliation that was heaped on Charles Thomas."

No major league team had hired a black player since 1884. African Americans played top-notch baseball in the Negro Leagues, but they but did not receive the salaries or recognition they deserved. Rickey wanted to right this injustice.

In Jackie Robinson he found a fine player who had the courage and dignity to withstand the insults and threats of racists. Although the pressure on him was intense, Robinson became a leading player for the Dodgers. Soon, black players joined other teams, and the color line disappeared.

Golfer Jack Nicklaus, who was born in Columbus in 1940, also charmed many fans. Sportswriter Glenn Dickey has called Nicklaus "an artist" who "plays golf better than anyone who ever lived."

*The "Golden Bear," Jack Nicklaus, lines up a putt.*

At Ohio State University, Nicklaus majored in pharmacy and worked in his father's drugstores during vacations. But his golfing talent led Nicklaus to turn pro in 1959 after he won his second big amateur title. At age twenty-one, he won his first U.S. Open tournament. During the 1960s and 1970s, Nicklaus was the top male professional golfer and the sport's all-time money winner. In 1986, he won his seventy-first lifetime title in a dramatic one-stroke victory at the Masters Tournament.

Phoebe Anne Moses, better known as Annie Oakley, was born in a log cabin in Darke County, Ohio, in 1860. As a child, she learned to hunt rabbits and other game in order to feed her family. When she was fifteen years old, she won her first shooting contest.

Her impressive skills earned her a place in a vaudeville show. Using the name Annie Oakley, she toured America. Later, she traveled the world with Buffalo Bill's Wild West Show, astonishing audiences with her amazing sharpshooting skills. She performed stunts on horseback and hit dimes tossed in the air. The Sioux chief Sitting Bull called her Little Sure Shot.

During World War I, Oakley entertained soldiers at military camps and visited veterans hospitals. Although she was sixty-two years old, she could still hit a hundred targets in a row. *Annie Get Your Gun*, a Broadway musical that later became a film, was based on her extraordinary life.

Rising from Ohio's towns and cities, people from the Buckeye State have gone on to excel in every area of life. They have made their mark in the world and even on the surface of the moon.

*Sharpshooter Annie Oakley, a Quaker, often read the Bible and never used her weapon against another human being.*

# 6 GOING FAR IN OHIO

**O**hio has something for everyone. Curious minds can explore the history of flight, pottery, or rock and roll. Thrill seekers can ride the world's largest roller coaster or brave six-foot-high columns of water at the Wave in Geauga Lake. More than 60 million nature lovers visit Ohio's seventy-two state parks each year. Travel writer Barbara Leskey tells her fellow Ohioans, "Stay where you are, and yet go far."

## THE NORTHWEST

One of Ohio's most exciting regions is western Lake Erie near Sandusky and Toledo. Sandusky is the home of Cedar Point, one of the nation's largest and most popular amusement parks. A big attraction there is the Mantis, billed as "the world's tallest, fastest, steepest, standup coaster." Riders race up and down the 3,900-foot track at speeds up to sixty miles per hour.

The park features tamer rides and fun for small children. Visitors under four feet tall enjoy Berenstain Bear Country, with characters and buildings taken from the popular children's books. The Oceana aquarium includes dolphins, sharks, and other sea creatures. Nearby Soak City features more than a dozen water slides and other attractions.

The Bass Islands draw thousands of tourists each year. Middle

*Thrilling rides await visitors at Cedar Point, which also features theaters, animal attractions, and a beach.*

Bass Island features a winery in a castlelike setting. Each year, barbershop quartets from around the nation gather to perform here. On neighboring South Bass is Put-in-Bay, which has a beautiful Victorian main street and a monument to Commodore Perry's famous naval victory. A Cleveland resident says, "It wouldn't be summer for us without a trip to Put-in-Bay. We bike all around, stopping to fish, hike, and to have picnics on the beach." Fishing for walleyes, bass, islanders, and minnies is a popular pastime here.

On Kelleys Island you can see the glacial grooves, gullies etched into the earth by glaciers 30,000 years ago. The island also has a rock inscribed with ancient Indian drawings, some of animals and others of humans smoking pipes.

Toledo, near the Michigan border, is noted for its art museum, which houses a fine collection of ancient, American, and European art, including works by the famous European painters El Greco and Picasso. It also includes a great Egyptian collection with a real mummy.

## CLEVELAND: "ONE HOT CITY"

Ohio's second-largest city celebrated its bicentennial in 1996 by calling itself "one hot city." Cleveland features great restaurants and cafés, shopping areas, movie palaces, and cultural attractions. Landmark buildings include the fifty-two-story Terminal Tower, Ohio's second-tallest building. From its observation deck, you can see all around the city and out over Lake Erie. The Great Lakes Science Center features many hands-on exhibits, a five-story OMNIMAX theater, and a copy of NASA's mission control center in Houston.

The Cleveland Museum of Natural History has dinosaur skeletons, bird exhibits, and a gem room full of colorful precious stones and crystals. Many children are especially interested in the museum's exhibit about Balto, the heroic Alaskan sled dog who was featured in a 1995 film of the same name.

*At the annual historical weekend at Put-in-Bay, visitors can see authentic nineteenth-century naval uniforms and ships.*

## BUCKEYE MUSHERS

Most people associate sled-dog racing with Alaska, but each year Ohio hosts the Buckeye Classic Sled Dog Race. In 1996, thousands of spectators saw sixty teams compete.

Jona Stokes, an Ohio sled-dog racer, has helped promote this sport in the state and throughout the country. Stokes lives in Burton, where she and her husband raise huskies. She helped develop the Balto exhibit at the Cleveland Museum of Natural History. Balto was one of the brave Alaskan sled dogs who ran legs of a 674-mile trip in the middle of winter in 1925 to bring life-saving medicine to people in Nome, Alaska, who had been stricken by diphtheria.

Stokes is also part of Mush With Pride, an organization that teaches people how to properly care for and train sled dogs. She writes articles about her sport and enjoys speaking to young people, often at schools. Some of her talks include live demonstrations with sled dogs. Stokes says, "I tell children not only about the joys of my sport but about the many things they can do outdoors, like hiking, backpacking, or going on a winter picnic. We need to get away from the television and explore the wonders outdoors. It's all out there waiting."

# TEN LARGEST CITIES

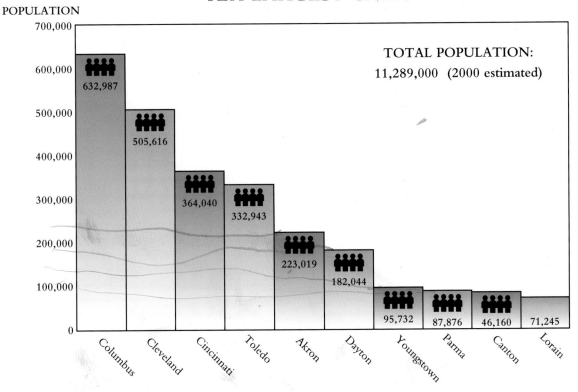

POPULATION

TOTAL POPULATION:
11,289,000  (2000 estimated)

700,000

600,000 — 632,987 (Columbus)

500,000 — 505,616 (Cleveland)

400,000

300,000 — 364,040 (Cincinnati), 332,943 (Toledo)

200,000 — 223,019 (Akron), 182,044 (Dayton)

100,000 — 95,732 (Youngstown), 87,876 (Parma), 46,160 (Canton), 71,245 (Lorain)

0

Columbus  Cleveland  Cincinnati  Toledo  Akron  Dayton  Youngstown  Parma  Canton  Lorain

Tourists from all over the world visit Cleveland to see the Rock and Roll Hall of Fame and Museum. The museum offers visitors a chance to hear the five hundred most important rock songs of all time and learn about the artists who wrote and performed them. The collection includes musical instruments, handwritten lyrics, and other rock memorabilia, such as a black leather costume worn by Elvis Presley. "Our whole family liked the Hall of Fame, including my grandma who is an Elvis fan," says a teenage visitor. "You'd have to go there more than once to see everything."

*The Rock and Roll Hall of Fame is located in Cleveland, where the world's first rock concert was held in 1952. One year earlier, Cleveland deejay Alan Freed had coined the term "rock and roll."*

## THE EAST

South of Cleveland is one of Ohio's big industrial regions. Akron is home to the Goodyear World of Rubber, where visitors learn about the material that enriched this city. Exhibits explain how rubber got its start in Charles Goodyear's kitchen and how it has been used in everything from artificial hearts to blimps. You can even see how tires are made.

Canton is home to the Pro Football Hall of Fame, which honors top players, coaches, and others who have contributed to the game. At the entrance is a statue of Jim Thorpe, an Olympic gold medalist who played for the Canton Bulldogs in the 1920s. Each summer, the hall welcomes new honorees with a parade and ceremony. The Canton Classic Car Museum features more than thirty beautifully restored antique cars, along with automobile memorabilia from days gone by.

*Fans can learn all about their favorite teams at the Pro Football Hall of Fame.*

South of Canton, history lives on near New Philadelphia, where the restored village of Schoenbrunn offers a glimpse of late-eighteenth-century life. Schoenbrunn began as a Christian mission for the Delaware Indians but was abandoned during the American Revolution. In 1923, the Ohio Historical Society bought the land and set out to rebuild Schoenbrunn. Today, tour guides wearing eighteenth-century dress show visitors around the village. The church and log cabins include pieces of the original buildings, as does the one-room schoolhouse, with its straight, backless wooden benches and stone fireplace. For summer visitors, an outdoor drama, *The Trumpet in the Land*, tells the story of Ohio's first Christian settlement.

The Museum of Ceramics in East Liverpool examines the history of the area's pottery, porcelain, bone china, and glass industries. Each June, the Tri-State Pottery Festival features pottery displays, contests, tours of local plants, antiques, and art shows.

The twenty-one restored homes and buildings at Hale Farm and Village in Bath give a good idea about what life was like on an Ohio farm in the early nineteenth century. Artisans and craftspeople demonstrate glassblowing, carpentry, blacksmithing, spinning, and candle making.

Not far from Canton in northeastern Ohio is Amish country, a quiet farming area where people still live a simple life, without many technological conveniences. The Amish towns feature shops selling homemade crafts and tools. Delicious foods can be bought at the restaurants, cheese factories, and bake shops. Visitors leave with packages of green moon cheese, maple sugar candy, and gooey shoofly pie, which has a molasses filling. Colorful handmade Amish quilts are also popular.

*Handmade candles dry before a stone fireplace inside one of the eighteenth-century cabins at Schoenbrunn State Memorial.*

## COLUMBUS

Columbus, on the east bank of the Scioto River, became Ohio's capital in 1812. The old brick and stone statehouse burned down in 1961 just as the new one was being built. The new building, which has four grand columned entrances, is one of the few state capitols that has no dome.

A great downtown attraction is the full-scale replica of the *Santa Maria*, the ship Christopher Columbus sailed to America. While you visit the boat, costumed guides tell you what life was like on the long journey across the ocean. At Ohio's Center of Science & Industry, more than a thousand exhibits make science fun. Both adults and children enjoy hands-on activities, such as hopping onto the keys of a large computer, riding a high-wire bicycle, or climbing inside a genuine 1961 Mercury space capsule. You can also explore a model coal mine to learn about Ohio's industrial heritage.

The Franklin Park Conservatory & Botanical Garden contains a

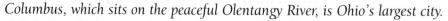

*Columbus, which sits on the peaceful Olentangy River, is Ohio's largest city.*

magnificent collection of plants—more than 1,200 different kinds—from around the world and from climates ranging from desert to mountains to rain forest. Another great Columbus site offers a different way to appreciate plants. At the Topiary Garden in Old Deaf School Park, huge shrubs are trimmed to resemble people, dogs, monkeys, and even boats. Summer visitors to Columbus can refresh themselves at Wyandot Adventure Park, which has a million-gallon wave pool, seventy-foot water slides, and many other great rides, both wet and dry.

History can be discovered at some former stations on the Underground Railroad, which are open to the public. Among them are the Platt log cabin in West Liberty, northwest of Columbus, and the home of Reverend John Rankin in Ripley in southern Ohio. Rankin hid more than two thousand runaways between 1825 and 1865. Many older homes in Ohio have secret rooms that were used to hide runaways.

## THE SOUTH

Prehistoric mound-building cultures lived south of present-day Columbus. The Hopewell Culture National Historic Park is located near Chillicothe. People of the Hopewell culture built burial mounds at this site more than two thousand years ago. Farther south is the amazing Great Serpent Mound, which has impressed scientists from around the world. Visitors to the Leo Petroglyph site in Jackson walk along trails past a ravine to view rocks with dozens of pictures of people, birds, and animals. The meaning of these Native American drawings remains a mystery.

# PLACES TO SEE

Lake Erie

Headlands Beach State Park

Ashtabula

Pymatuning Reservoir

Cedar Point

Toledo

Cleveland

The Rock and Roll Hall of Fame & Museum

Fort Meigs

Lorain

Parma

Shenango River Lake

Sandusky

Sea World of Ohio

Warren

Bowling Green

Maumee R.

Auglaize R.

Findlay

Akron

Youngstown

Berlin Lake

Alliance

Lima

Sandusky R.

Massillon

Canton

Marion

Mansfield

Charles Mill Lake

Killbuck R.

Sugar R.

East Liverpool

Indian Lake

Scioto R.

Ohio's Amish Country

Zoar Village

Grand Lake St. Marys

Campbell Hill
▲ (1,549 ft.)

Steubenville

Tuscarawas R.

Ohio R.

Alum Creek L.

Newark

Dillon Lake

Cambridge

Great Miami R.

Ohio Historical Center

Licking R.

Zanesville

Springfield

Columbus

Buckeye Lake

The Wilds

U.S. Air Force Museum

Lancaster

Muskingum R.

Dayton

Middletown

Hocking Hills State Park

Marietta

Cincinnati

Mound City Group National Monument

Chillicothe

Athens

Museum Center

Paint R.

Rocky Fork Lake

Serpent Mound

Scioto R.

Ohio R.

Ohio R.

Portsmouth

Southeast of Columbus is Dayton, the birthplace of aviation. The Aviation Hall of Fame honors the scientists, inventors, pilots, and engineers who helped men and women get off the ground. The United States Air Force Museum, at Wright-Patterson Air Force Base, contains the world's oldest and most complete military aviation collection. On display are B-29s, many other fighter planes, and an Apollo space capsule.

Farther south along the western Ohio River is Cincinnati. History lovers can sample the nineteenth century at Sharon Woods Village or examine documents and objects from the days of slavery at the Harriet Beecher Stowe House. The Arts Consortium African American Museum traces the history of blacks in the city. The dramatic history of fire fighting is shown at the Cincinnati Fire Museum, which is located in a restored 1907 fire station. Although some people think the highlight of this museum is an 1884 steam-powered fire engine, others prefer the chance to slide down a fire pole.

The Cincinnati Zoo is famous for having the world's most comprehensive collection of wild cats—nineteen different species in all. Another highlight is its Jungle Trails rain forest exhibit, where orangutans and other primates can cavort.

The Cincinnati Art Museum has an outstanding Native American collection, as well as art from around the world. Visitors to the Cincinnati Museum of Natural History can explore full-sized replicas of Ohio caves. One contains a thirty-foot waterfall and intricate mineral formations. You can also visit a simulated glacier.

Marietta, the first permanent white settlement in Ohio, is steeped in history. In this charming town, you can hop on a trolley to get to the many historic homes and buildings. The Campus Martius

Museum features artifacts such as furniture and tools from the pioneer days. At the museum, you can even amble through Ohio's oldest house and imagine how these brave settlers lived.

Visitors to Marietta can also enjoy a ride on the *Valley Gem*, one of the last sternwheeler riverboats still operating on an inland waterway. The Ohio River Museum contains an authentic sternwheeler, the *W. P. Snyder*, and other exhibits that bring to life the bygone days of the steamboat. Although another sternwheeler, the *Becky Thatcher*, never leaves port, people flock to it anyway to enjoy a dramatic play while eating dinner.

These are just a few of the places that invite visitors to explore Ohio's history, meet famous people of past and present, and glimpse the future while learning about science and industry. "We have some of the biggest, the best, and most beautiful things here," a proud Ohioan says of his state. "Our family has had great times right in our own backyard."

*In many cities, including Cincinnati, sternwheelers remind visitors of the region's colorful past.*

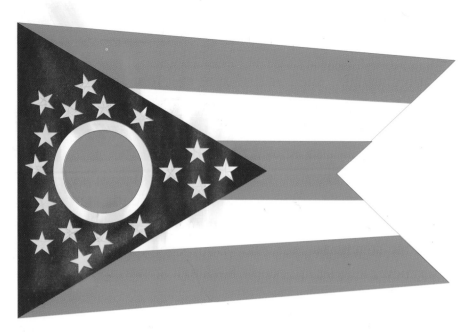

THE FLAG: The tips on the pennant-shaped flag stand for Ohio's hills and valleys, while the red and white stripes represent its roads and waterways. On the blue triangle, the white circle with the red center stands for both the O in Ohio and the buckeye nut. The 17 stars indicate Ohio was the seventeenth state to enter the Union. The flag was adopted in 1902.

THE SEAL: Adopted in 1967, the state seal shows the Scioto River running between Mount Logan and a field of wheat. In the field is a bundle of 17 arrows, again representing Ohio's place as the seventeenth state. A bundle of wheat, showing the importance of agriculture, stands next to the arrows. In the background, the sun rises, casting 17 rays over the mountain, symbolizing Ohio being the first state west of the Allegheny Mountains.

# STATE SURVEY

**Statehood:** March 1, 1803

**Origin of Name:** Ohio is named after the Ohio River. The Iroquois Indians called the river the *O-hy-o*, which means "something great."

**Nickname:** Buckeye State

**Capital:** Columbus

**Motto:** With God, All Things Are Possible

**Animal:** White-tailed deer

**Beverage:** Tomato juice

**Bird:** Cardinal

**Flower:** Scarlet carnation

**Fossil:** Trilobite

**Insect:** Ladybug

**Reptile:** Black racer (snake)

*Ladybug*

# BEAUTIFUL OHIO

This perennially favorite waltz was written in 1918 and adopted as the official state song in 1969. In 1989, new lyrics were composed, changing the feeling from an old-fashioned love song to an expression of affection for the whole state.

**Words by Wilbert B. McBride**　　　　　　　　　**Music by Mary Earl**

*Trillium*

**Stone:** Flint

**Tree:** Buckeye

**Wildflower:** Trillium

## GEOGRAPHY

**Highest Point:** 1,550 feet above sea level at Campbell Hill in Logan County

**Lowest Point:** 433 feet above sea level at the intersection of the Ohio and Miami Rivers in Hamilton County

**Area:** 41,328 square miles

**Greatest Distance, North to South:** 245 miles

**Greatest Distance, East to West:** 227 miles

**Bordering States:** Michigan to the north, Pennsylvania and West Virginia to the east, West Virginia and Kentucky to the south, and Indiana to the west

**Hottest Recorded Temperature:** 113°F at Gallipolis on July 21, 1934

**Coldest Recorded Temperature:** -39°F at Milligan on February 10, 1899

**Average Annual Precipitation:** 38 inches

**Major Rivers:** Auglaize, Chagrin, Cuyahoga, Grand, Great Miami, Hocking, Huron, Little Miami, Maumee, Muskingum, Ohio, Olentangy, Portage, Sandusky, Scioto, Tuscawaras, Vermilion

**Major Lakes**: Alum Creek, Berlin, Buckeye, Burr Oak, Caesar Creek, Dillon, Erie, Grand Lake St. Marys, Indian, Mosquito Creek, Piedmont, Rocky Fork, Salt Fork, Senecaville, Tappan

**Trees**: ash, beech, birch, buckeye, chestnut, cottonwood, crabtree, cypress, dogwood, elm, fir, hemlock, hickory, larch, locust, magnolia, maple, oak, Osage orange, pawpaw, pine, poplar, redbud, sassafras, spruce, sumac, sweetgum, sycamore, tulip tree, walnut, willow

**Wild Plants**: aster, black-eyed Susan, bluebell, buttercup, coneflower, Dutchman's-breeches, field daisy, ginseng, goldenrod, golden seal, ironweed, jack-in-the-pulpit, lady's slippers, marsh marigold, mayapple, milkweed, mountain laurel, pitcher plant, rhododendron, shooting star, squirrel corn, sunflower, trillium, wild carrot, wild columbine, wild geranium, wild lily, wild rose, wood lily

**Animals**: beaver, chipmunk, coyote, eastern cottontail rabbit, gray fox, groundhog, mink, muskrat, opossum, raccoon, skunk, squirrel, weasel, white fox, white-tailed deer

*Weasel*

**Birds**: blackbird, Canada goose, cardinal, cowbird, dove, duck, finch, grouse, gull, hawk, heron, hummingbird, mockingbird, nuthatch, owl, pheasant, sparrow, starling, swallow, swan, thrush, vulture, whippoor-will, woodpecker, wren

**Fish:** bluegill, carp, catfish, gar, largemouth bass, muskellunge, northern pike, perch, sheephead, smallmouth bass, sucker, sunfish, trout, walleye, white bass

**Endangered Animals:** bald eagle, barn owl, bobcat, Canada warbler, cave salamander, common tern, eastern plains garter snake, eastern salamander, golden-winged warbler, green salamander, Indiana bat, Kirtland's warbler, least bittern, loggerhead shrike, magnolia warbler, northern copperbelly, northern harrier, peregrine falcon, piping plover, river otter, sandhill crane, sharp-shinned hawk, spotted turtle, upland sandpiper, winter wren

*Northern harrier*

**Endangered Plants:** northern wild monkshood, lakeside daisy, eastern prairie fringed orchid, running buffalo clover

## TIMELINE

Ohio History

700 B.C. The Adena begin building mounds in what is today southern Ohio

A.D. 1500 Shawnees, Miamis, Wyandots, Mingos, and Delawares live in present-day Ohio

1669 Frenchman René-Robert Cavelier, Sieur de La Salle, is the first European to see the Ohio region

1745 The British build their first fort in Ohio on Sandusky Bay

1749 Celoron de Blainville of France travels through the Ohio Valley, claiming the area for his country

1763 After its defeat in the French and Indian War, France gives up most of its territory in North America, including the Ohio region

1763 Native Americans attack British forts along the Great Lakes, capturing Fort Sandusky

1772 David Zeisberger founds the Schoenbrunn mission to shelter Christian Indians

1773 The first school west of the Appalachian Mountains opens at Schoenbrunn

1775 The American Revolution begins

1787 Ohio becomes part of the Northwest Territory, which will eventually become five states

1788 Marietta, the first permanent white settlement in Ohio, is founded

1793 The first newspaper in the Northwest Territory, the *Centinel of the North-Western Territory*, is published in Cincinnati

1794 At the Battle of Fallen Timbers, U.S. troops defeat Native American forces, ending Indian resistance to settlement in Ohio

1796 Cleveland is founded by Moses Cleaveland

1803 Ohio becomes the 17th state; the first state capital is Chillicothe

1813 During the War of 1812, American ships under the command of Lieutenant Oliver Hazard Perry defeat a British fleet in the Battle of Lake Erie near Put-in-Bay

1816 Columbus becomes the state capital

1835 Ohio and the Michigan Territory argue over the boundary line between the two, leading to the Toledo War

1837 Ohio's first railroad, a horse-drawn train, operates between Toledo and Adrian, Michigan

1845 The Miami and Erie Canal, between Cincinnati and Toledo, is completed

1861–1865 The Civil War is fought; over 300,000 Ohioans fight for the Union

1868 Civil War hero and native Ohioan Ulysses S. Grant is elected president of the United States

1869 America's first professional baseball team, the Cincinnati Red Stockings, is formed

1913 Some 430 people die in the worst flooding in the history of the state

1941–1945 America fights in World War II; about 840,000 Ohio men and women serve in the armed forces

1955 The Ohio Turnpike is completed

**1967** Carl B. Stokes becomes the first African American to lead a major American city when he is elected mayor of Cleveland

**1970** National Guard troops kill four students at Kent State University during protests against the Vietnam War

**1974** A tornado kills 35 people in Xenia and destroys much of the town

**1995** The Rock and Roll Hall of Fame and Museum opens in Cleveland

## ECONOMY

**Agricultural Products:** apples, celery, corn, cucumbers, dairy products, eggs, grapes, hay, hogs, mushrooms, oats, onions, peaches, potatoes, poultry, rye, sheep, soybeans, strawberries, sugar beets, sweet corn, tobacco, tomatoes, wheat

*Hogs*

**Manufactured Products:** automobiles, chemicals, electrical equipment, furniture, glass products, industrial machinery, metals, paper products, processed foods, rubber products, trucks and buses, wood products

**Natural Resources:** clay, coal, gypsum, limestone, natural gas, peat, petroleum, salt, sand and gravel, sandstone, shale

**Business and Trade:** communications, finance, insurance, printing and publishing, real estate, retail trade, tourism, transportation, wholesale trade

## CALENDAR OF CELEBRATIONS

**Winter Games** The games that were played by Ohio's pioneers and Native Americans in the cold of winter are featured in this February festival, held at the Flint Ridge State Memorial near Glenford. Visitors can throw a spear through a rolling hoop, toss a corncob arrow, or build a snowman. You can also try your hand at making a shell necklace or flint arrowhead.

**St. Patrick's Day Parade and Celebration** What better place to be a little Irish on St. Patrick's Day than in Dublin? This central Ohio city celebrates the March holiday starting with a pancake breakfast and parade, followed by plenty of Irish food, music, and fun.

**U. S. Grant's Birthday Celebration** Point Pleasant and Georgetown commemorate Ulysses S. Grant's birthday in late April. During the celebration you can tour his birthplace and boyhood homes and see a re-enactment of life in a Civil War camp.

**The Great Fossil Hunt** Held in May at Caesar Creek State Park near Waynesville, this event celebrates the area's abundant fossils. Park rangers are on hand to help you hunt for and identify the fossils of tiny sea animals.

**Festival of the Fish** The bounty of Lake Erie is celebrated with food and music during this June festival in Vermilion. Wacky boat races as well as an evening parade of boats are held on the Vermilion River.

**Old Northwest Territory Primitive Rendezvous** The explorers, pioneers, fur trappers, and Native Americans of early Ohio come to life during this June event in Springfield. Costumed actors demonstrate what it was like when frontier people came together to trade and celebrate. You can sample foods of the era and view arts and crafts demonstrations.

**Great Mohican Indian Powwow** Native Americans from all over the United States come together at Loudonville for this July festival. You can watch Native American dancers, sample authentic foods, and listen to story-telling.

**Dayton Air Show** Considered the finest air show in the country, this July event features the very best of the aviation world. Watch the skies as pilots perform death-defying aerobatics or stroll the grounds of the Dayton International Airport to get a close-up look at modern and historical aircraft.

**Pro Football Hall of Fame Festival** Canton celebrates its football heritage with a weeklong festival in July just before the new Hall of Fame members are inducted. There's a grand parade, a drum corps competition, and lots of food. The week ends with two pro teams playing in the Hall of Fame Game.

**Ohio State Fair** If you like your good times to be big, you'll love the Ohio State Fair in Columbus. Every August, 20,000 farm animals are brought in to compete for prizes. Besides touring the animal barns, you can check out the life-size butter sculptures in the dairy barn, enjoy thrill rides, listen to music, and eat great fair food.

*Ohio State Fair*

**Ohio Renaissance Festival** Travel back to the days of knights and fair maidens during this festival held near Waynesville each August. At a replica of a 16th-century English village, you can watch jousting and storytelling, sample medieval foods, and dance to minstrel music.

**Ohio Swiss Festival** Locally made Swiss cheese is the star at this Amish country celebration held every August in Sugarcreek. There's also Swiss music, polka dancing, sporting events, and a parade.

**German Village Oktoberfest** Held every September in Columbus's German Village, an authentic 19th-century German immigrant neighborhood, this Oktoberfest has everything you'd expect. You can fill up on German foods, from bratwursts to cream puffs, then dance to the music of oompah-pah bands.

**Pumpkin Show** Ever seen a pumpkin pie that's five feet across? How about a pumpkin that weighs over 400 pounds? Those are just a few of the attractions at this October festival in Circleville. You can sample pumpkin fudge or pumpkin burgers, or try your hand at the pumpkin-carving contest. The celebration also includes rides, music, and parades.

**Covered Bridge Festival** The more than a dozen covered bridges near Ashtabula are celebrated every October with a parade, draft-horse pulls, a plowing contest, and covered bridge tours. There's also food and live entertainment.

**International Festival** Cultures from around the world are highlighted at this exciting festival. During this November celebration in Columbus, you can discover the food, music, and crafts of more than 60 nationalities.

## STATE STARS

**Neil Armstrong** (1930–    ), of Wapakoneta, was the first person to walk on the moon. Armstrong was the commander of the *Apollo 11* mission, when he set foot on the moon on July 16, 1969.

**Erma Bombeck** (1927–1996) earned fame for writing humorous newspaper columns on the trials of everyday life and parenthood. She also authored a number of best-selling books, including *The Grass Is Always Greener over the Septic Tank* and *If Life Is a Bowl of Cherries, What Am I Doing in the Pits?* Bombeck was born in Dayton.

*Erma Bombeck*

**Charles Chestnutt** (1858–1932), a noted African-American writer, was born in Cleveland. His works often explored prejudice, and he was one of the first writers to portray blacks realistically and sensitively. Chestnutt's works included *The Conjure Woman* and *The House Behind the Cedars*.

**George Armstrong Custer** (1839–1876) was born in New Rumley. He first achieved fame as a Union cavalry officer during the Civil War. Following the war, Custer fought against the Plains Indians and was killed during the Battle of the Little Bighorn in Montana.

**Clarence Darrow** (1857–1938), one of America's greatest defense lawyers, was born in Kinsman. Darrow's most famous case was the Scopes "monkey trial," in which he defended a teacher accused of teaching the theory of evolution.

*Clarence Darrow*

**Charles Gates Dawes** (1865–1951), a Marietta native, spent much of his life in public service. In 1925, he won the Nobel Peace Prize for his plan to restore the economy of Germany following World War I. Dawes served as vice president of the United States under President Calvin Coolidge and as U.S. ambassador to Britain.

**Rita Dove** (1952–     ), of Akron, is an accomplished poet. Her poetry collection *Thomas and Beulah* won the Pulitzer Prize. In 1993, Dove

became the first African American, and the youngest person ever, to be named Poet Laureate of the United States.

*Rita Dove*

**Paul Laurence Dunbar** (1872–1906) earned fame for his poetry and novels, which were often written in African-American dialect. His works included *Lyrics of Lowly Life* and *The Sport of the Gods*. Dunbar was born in Dayton.

*Paul Laurence Dunbar*

**Thomas Alva Edison** (1847–1931), who was born in Milan, was one of the world's greatest inventors. He was the only American inventor to hold more than 1,000 patents. Edison's inventions include the electric light bulb, the phonograph, and the motion picture projector.

**Clark Gable** (1901–1960), a native of Cadiz, was a well-known movie star. He won an Academy Award for his performance in *It Happened One Night*. His most popular role was that of Rhett Butler in *Gone with the Wind*.

**John Glenn** (1921–    ), was the first American to orbit Earth. Glenn had been a fighter pilot in both World War II and the Korean War. As a test pilot, he was the first person to fly across the United States at supersonic speed. Then, in 1962, he made his brief historic flight around the earth. Later Glenn, who was born in Cambridge, served as a U.S. senator from Ohio from 1975 to 1998.

**Ulysses S. Grant** (1822–1885) was the 18th president of the United States. Born in Point Pleasant, Grant gained fame as a Union general during the Civil War, winning many victories along the Mississippi River, including the capture of Vicksburg, Mississippi, in 1863. He later became the commander of all Union military forces during the war.

**Zane Grey** (1872–1939) has been called the Father of the Adult Western. His numerous novels include *Riders of the Purple Sage*, *Call of the Canyon*, and *The Thundering Herd*. Grey was born in Zanesville.

**Arsenio Hall** (1958–    ), born in Cleveland, was the first African American to host a successful late-night talk show. *The Arsenio Hall Show* ran from 1989 to 1993. Hall has appeared in several movies, including *Coming to America*.

*Arsenio Hall*

**Bob Hope** (1903–    ) moved to Cleveland at age four. Starting off in vaudeville, Hope went on to star in many successful comedy films, such as *Road to Singapore*, *Road to Rio*, and *Call Me Bwaana*. He later hosted a series of popular television specials. Hope is well known for entertaining American military forces all around the world, during both peace and war.

**Charles F. Kettering** (1876–1958), of Loudonville, is credited with many important inventions. After creating the electric cash register, Kettering came up with his most famous invention, the electric starter for automobiles. He also invented safety glass, fast-drying automobile paint, and a fuel injection system for diesel engines. He served as the director of research for General Motors for many years.

**Maya Lin** (1959–    ) was only 21 years old when her design was chosen for the Vietnam Veterans Memorial in Washington, D.C. Her monument, a black granite wall inscribed with the names of the war's dead, is a popular and emotional attraction. The young artist, who was born in Athens, also designed the Civil Rights Memorial in Montgomery, Alabama.

*Maya Lin*

**Toni Morrison** (1931–    ) writes about the struggles of African-American women. Her works include *Song of Solomon* and *Beloved*, which won a Pulitzer Prize in 1988. In 1993, she became the first African-American woman to receive the Nobel Prize for literature. Morrison was born in Lorain.

**Paul Newman** (1925–    ) is one of America's most popular movie actors. His films include *The Hustler*, *Cool Hand Luke*, *Butch Cassidy and the Sundance Kid*, *The Sting*, and *The Color of Money*. In recent years, Newman, who was born in Shaker Heights, has marketed a line of gourmet food items, such as salad dressing and popcorn. The profits go to charity.

**Jack Nicklaus** (1940–    ), a Columbus native, is one of the greatest professional golfers of all time. Nicklaus won the Masters Tournament a record six times and the U.S. Open four times. He was elected to the World Golf Hall of Fame in 1974. Nicklaus has also designed golf courses all around the world.

**Jesse Owens** (1913–1980) moved to Cleveland as a young boy. As a track star at Ohio State University, he set a number of world records. In the 1936 summer Olympics in Berlin, Germany, Owens won four gold medals: in the 100-meter and 200-meter dashes, the long jump, and the men's relay. Because Owens was black, his victories embarrassed Nazi leader Adolf Hitler, who had hoped to use the Olympics as a showcase for his theories of white supremacy.

**Pete Rose** (1941–    ), one of baseball's greats, was born in Cincinnati and spent much of his career with the Cincinnati Reds. As a player-manager for the Reds in 1985, he broke the all-time hitting record of 4,191 held by Ty Cobb.

**William Tecumseh Sherman** (1820–1891) was one of the greatest generals to emerge from the Civil War. His "March to the Sea" through Georgia in 1864 helped destroy the South's will to fight on. He later became the commanding general of the army. Sherman was born in Lancaster.

*William Tecumseh Sherman*

**Steven Spielberg** (1947–     ), the director of many blockbuster films, was born in Cincinnati. His hits have included *E.T.: The Extraterrestrial*, *Raiders of the Lost Ark*, *Jurassic Park*, and *Schindler's List*.

**Gloria Steinem** (1934–     ), born in Toledo, is one of the country's leading activists for women's rights. She helped found *Ms.* magazine in 1972 and has continued to write and lecture on behalf of women's rights.

**R. L. Stine** (1943–     ) has made a career out of scaring the wits out of children. His *Goosebumps* book series, introduced in the early 1990s, has sold millions of copies. The stories even became a popular television series. Stine is a native of Bexley.

**Carl B. Stokes** (1927–     ) was born in Cleveland. When he was chosen to lead that city in 1967, he became the first African American elected mayor of a major American city. Later, Stokes served as the U.S. ambassador to the Seychelles, an island nation in the Indian Ocean.

**William Howard Taft** (1857–1930) was the 27th president of the United States. Born in Cincinnati, Taft served as a judge, territorial governor of the Philippines, and U.S. secretary of war before becoming president. After his presidency, Taft became chief justice of the U.S. Supreme Court, which made him the only ex-president to serve on the court.

**Tecumseh** (1768–1813), a Shawnee chief, was born near what is today the town of Xenia. One of the greatest Native American leaders, Tecumseh hoped to unite all North America Indians against the whites. He was killed in battle after siding with the British during the War of 1812.

**James Thurber** (1894–1961), humorist and author, was born in Columbus. Best known for his short story "The Secret Life of Walter Mitty," Thurber also wrote the books *My Life and Hard Times*, *The Thurber Carnival*, and *The Beast in Me and Other Animals*.

**Orville** (1871–1948) and **Wilbur Wright** (1867–1912) of Dayton made the world's first successful airplane flight. The brothers flew their motor-powered aircraft on December 17, 1903, at Kitty Hawk, North Carolina.

## TOUR THE STATE

**Toledo Museum of Art** (Toledo) At this world-famous art collection, you can see everything from an Egyptian mummy and African sculpture to French furniture and American glassware.

**Kelleys Island** (Kelleys Island) You can only reach this resort island in Lake Erie by boat, but it's worth the trip to see some of Ohio's ancient history. Inscription Rock is covered with picture drawings made by prehistoric

Indians. The Glacial Grooves in Kelleys Island State Park were carved in solid stone by huge moving walls of ice more than 30,000 years ago.

**Thomas Edison Birthplace Museum** (Milan) The house where America's greatest inventor was born and lived as a boy looks much like it did in Edison's youth. Inside you can see replicas of Edison's greatest inventions.

**The Rock and Roll Hall of Fame and Museum** (Cleveland) The history of rock and roll is on display at this exciting lakefront museum. The guitars, clothes, and music of rock and roll's best are featured.

**Cleveland Metroparks Zoo** (Cleveland) More than 3,000 creatures call this zoo home. Many animals such as zebras, giraffes, ostriches, kangaroos, wallabies, and wolves are found in realistic outdoor environments. The rain forest exhibit contains 600 animals and 10,000 plants with a 25-foot waterfall and simulated thunderstorms.

*Fort Miegs*

**Headlands Beach State Park** (Mentor) Some of Lake Erie's best beaches are found in this park, which is great for swimming, playing, and picnicking. Nearby at the Mentor Marsh State Nature Preserve, there's also hiking and bird-watching.

**Cuyahoga Valley National Recreation Area** (Brecksville) Stretching along a 22-mile section of the Cuyahoga River, this park offers hiking, picnicking, biking, and canoeing. You can also explore old sections of the Ohio and Erie Canal where parts of the canal's locks and historic buildings still stand.

**Inventure Place** (Akron) Learn about America's greatest inventors at this museum's National Inventors Hall of Fame, where the creators of everything from the cotton gin to the videotape recorder are highlighted. You can also experiment with strobe lights and electromagnets at hands-on exhibits.

**Pro Football Hall of Fame** (Canton) The legends of the game come alive in the city where pro football started in 1920. Bronze statues showcase the game's best players. Exhibits feature everything from old uniforms to Super Bowl rings. You can also watch football's greatest moments on video.

**German Culture Museum** (Walnut Creek) This museum is one of the best places to learn about Ohio's large Amish community. Exhibits about the Amish and other Swiss-German peoples who settled in the region include fine examples of their furniture, quilts, and folk art.

**Schoenbrunn Village** (New Philadelphia) This reconstructed mission village looks much like it did in 1772 when it was founded as a home for Christian Indians. Today, you can sit on the wood benches in the village's school and church and explore small cabins and a graveyard.

**Campus Martius Museum** (Marietta) The oldest cabin in Ohio is on display at this museum, along with other artifacts dealing with the early settlement of the Northwest Territory.

**Hocking Hills State Park** (Logan) Spectacular cliffs, caves, and waterfalls are found throughout this popular spot for hiking and picnicking. The Conkles Hollow area features multicolored sandstone cliffs over 200 feet high. Rock House is a cliffside cave with a number of "windows" looking out into a gorge.

**Ohio Historical Center and Ohio Village** (Columbus) Trace Ohio's natural and human history with fun, hands-on exhibits at the historical center. You can test your knowledge with computer quizzes or touch a piece of petrified wood. Other displays include a giant mastodon skeleton and life-size replicas of Native American dwellings. Ohio Village is a re-creation of a 19th-century Ohio town, complete with a school, blacksmith shop, doctor's office, and other buildings.

**Hopewell Culture National Historical Park** (Chillicothe) Twenty-three cone-shaped mounds built by the Hopewell Indians more than a thousand years ago can be found at this site in southern Ohio. Walking trails lead throughout the mounds, and the visitor center contains displays on the Hopewell culture.

**Great Serpent Mound** (Peebles) One of the best preserved animal-shaped Indian mounds in the country, this curving snake is more than one-quarter of a mile long and about two thousand years old. You can walk around the entire mound or view it from an observation tower.

**National Afro-American Museum and Cultural Center** (Wilberforce) This museum focuses on the black experience in America. One exhibit features the history of African-American music, while another re-creates an African-American neighborhood from the 1950s.

**United States Air Force Museum** (Dayton) The more than 300 planes and missiles at this huge museum trace the history of the air force from its beginnings in the early 1900s to the present. You can see everything from the air force's very first planes to the massive B-36 bomber to the latest stealth fighter. You can also walk through the bomb bay of a nuclear bomber and sit in the cockpit of a modern jet fighter.

**Cedar Bog Nature Preserve** (Urbana) This unique bog is home to a number of rare and endangered plants and animals. From the boardwalk that twists through the preserve, you might glimpse a swamp rattlesnake, a spotted turtle, or an insect-eating sundew plant. The bog is also a good place for watching birds and butterflies.

**Neil Armstrong Air and Space Museum** (Wapakoneta) Dedicated to Ohio native Neil Armstrong, the first man on the moon, this museum traces the history of space travel. Displays include a jet fighter Armstrong flew as a test pilot and a Mercury space capsule. A sound tunnel and infinity room re-create what it feels like to be in space.

## FUN FACTS

Ever wonder why the city of Cleveland's name isn't spelled like that of its founder, Moses Cleaveland? In 1832, the editor of a local newspaper, the *Cleaveland Gazette and Commercial Register*, dropped the first "a" in "Cleaveland" so the title would fit on one line. The new spelling stuck.

Only in Zanesville would you get directions telling you to "go to the middle of the bridge and turn left." The city's famous Y-bridge is built at the intersection of the Muskingum and Licking Rivers. One span is built to the middle of the river, with spans forking to the left and right. It is believed to be the only Y-bridge in the world.

Annie Oakley, who was probably the best female sharpshooter ever, was born in Darke County. One day she hit 4,772 of 5,000 dimes and glass balls tossed in the air.

The first public library west of the Appalachian Mountains opened in Athens County in 1804. Called the Coonskin Library, it opened after two citizens took a wagonload of animal skins to Boston and returned with 51 books.

The little candy with the hole in the center, Life Savers, were invented in Cleveland in 1912. After his chocolate melted in the summer, candy-maker Clarence Crane made some hard mints, punched a hole in the middle of each, and sold them for five cents.

# FIND OUT MORE

If you want to find out more about Ohio, check your local library or bookstore for these titles:

## GENERAL STATE BOOKS

Brown, Dottie. *Ohio*. Minneapolis: Lerner, 1993.

Fradin, Dennis. *Ohio*. Chicago: Children's Press, 1993.

Wills, Charles A. *A Historical Album of Ohio*. Brookfield, CT: Millbrook Press, 1994.

## SPECIAL INTEREST BOOKS

Adler, David. *Jackie Robinson: He Was the First*. New York: Holiday House, 1989.

Cole, Michael D. *John Glenn, Astronaut and Senator*. Hillside, NJ: Enslow, 1993.

Herda, D.J. *Historical America: The North Central States*. Brookfield, CT: Millbrook Press, 1993.

Kent, Zachary. *The Civil War, "A House Divided."* Hillside, NJ: Enslow, 1994.

McKissack, Patricia and Fredrick McKissack. *Jesse Owens: Olympic Star.* Hillside, NJ: Enslow, 1993.

Macy, Sue. *A Whole New Ball Game.* New York: Henry Holt, 1993.

Tunis, Edward. *Frontier Living.* Cleveland: World, 1961.

## WEBSITES

http://www.ohiotourism.com

This website, Travel Ohio, gives hotel information and pictures and descriptions of important historical sites, museums, and other attractions.

# INDEX

Page numbers for charts, graphs, and illustrations are in boldface.